Bread Not Bombs

A Political Agenda for
Social Justice

The University of Alberta Press

Published by
The University of Alberta Press
Ring House 2
Edmonton, Alberta, Canada   T6G 2E1

Copyright © The University of Alberta Press 1999
Bread Not Bombs is a publication for the book trade from
The University of Alberta Press.

ISBN 0–88864–357–8

Canadian Cataloguing in Publication Data

Roche, Douglas, 1929–
  Bread not bombs

    ISBN 0–88864–357–8

    1. Social justice.   2. Peace.   I. Title
    HM671.R62 1999   303.3'72   C99–911095–0

∞ Printed on acid-free paper.
Printed and bound in Canada by Hignell Book Printing Ltd., Winnipeg, Manitoba.

The University of Alberta Press gratefully acknowledges the support received for
its publishing program from The Canada Council for the Arts. In addition, we
also gratefully acknowledge the financial support of the Government of Canada
through the Book Publishing Industry Development Program for our publishing
activities.

Canada

For my grandson
Nicholas Nolan Roche Hurley

Contents

Introduction

A Fateful Phone Call

On the Friday before Labour Day 1998, I was working on my computer at home, preparing for a speaking tour across Canada on the nuclear weapons issue. The phone rang, interrupting my concentration. An official of the Prime Minister's Office wanted to know the answer to a question: if the Prime Minister decided to appoint me a Senator, would I accept?

I found myself incredulous that the Prime Minister of Canada would invite me to become a Senator. I was content in my life as an educator and activist, and happy that, after 18 years in public life as a Member of Parliament and an Ambassador, I had recovered my freedom to speak, write, and teach my view of the human security agenda, unencumbered by party discipline and government policy. I thought I had seen the last of Parliament Hill and the Ottawa establishment.

Fifty years ago, when I left university, I became a journalist. My work took me through all the regions of the world, and I discovered the "global village." I wrote the life stories of a farmer in India, an Ibo teacher in Nigeria, a Communist labour leader in Venezuela. I found out that most of the world is nonwhite, non-Western and non-Christian, but that people everywhere, regardless of their background, wanted the same things: food, water, housing, work, and a chance to bring up their children in decency and hope.

In mid-life, in 1972, seeking a wider forum for my ideas about social justice, I ran and was elected to the House of Commons. In fact, I was elected four times and, caught in a cacophony of voices, tried to specialize in the areas of disarmament and development. I started going to the United Nations where I thought more serious work to alleviate the distresses of the human condition was being done than in Parliament. Frankly, I found the constraints of party discipline over-bearing.

I left Parliament of my own volition, determined to devote myself to the issues of disarmament and development. My timing was fortunate. The new Conservative government of 1984 needed an Ambassador for Disarmament. I accepted the appointment and worked for several years at the United Nations and a round of disarmament conferences in Geneva, Stockholm, and Vienna. I chaired the weekly meetings of the western nations at the U.N. throughout my tenure and, in 1988, was elected Chairman of the U.N. Disarmament Committee.

As the 1990s dawned, I felt the need to return to private life and was invited to become a Visiting Professor at the University of Alberta. I created my own 400-level seminar, "War or Peace in the 21st Century?" and found new vigour in challenging young—and very bright—minds to think about the conditions for peace in new ways that went beyond the rigidities of the "realism" school of political science. Being chosen by the student body as one of the best teachers at the University of Alberta reinforced my confidence that I could help a new generation discover a better road to peace and security.

I became involved in several nongovernmental organizations and founded a new body, the Middle Powers Initiative (MPI). MPI is a carefully focussed campaign, embracing prominent international citizens' organizations, to encourage the leaders of the Nuclear Weapons States to break free from their Cold War mindset and move rapidly to a nuclear-weapon-free world, which is now considered by many experts to be feasible.

Ten years after the supposed end of the Cold War, 35,000 nuclear weapons remain, and proliferation of weapons of mass destruction is spreading. The maintenance of nuclear weapons in the world today is an outrage against God and humanity. They are, as I have written previously, "the ultimate evil." The public has forgotten how calamitous for humanity a nuclear war would be.

Society accepts the presence of nuclear weapons because we accept violence. The 20th century was the bloodiest century in the history of humanity, with more than 110 million people killed in wars, three times as many people than all the war deaths in all the previous centuries from the first century A.D.

The killing record was maintained throughout the 1990s—Kosovo, Serbia, Bosnia, Northern Ireland, Haiti, The Congo, Rwanda, Burundi, Somalia, Mozambique, Afghanistan, Cambodia, Sri Lanka. These are just some of the countries from virtually all the regions of the world whose hopes for growth and prosperity were stifled by chronic conflicts.

The Gulf War in 1991 claimed more than 100,000 lives, cost $60 billion, and caused immense human suffering. More than 800,000 people were slaughtered in internecine warfare in Rwanda. NATO's bombing of Serbia and Kosovo, in response to atrocities and ethnic cleansing carried out by the Serbs, left a trail of destruction that will disrupt life into the next generation.

While wars are being fought, consuming vast amounts of resources, the world's poorest people are falling farther behind. During the past decade, inequalities have worsened throughout Asia, and poverty has skyrocketed in a crumbling Russia. Housing, health, and education services are desperately needed throughout the developing countries. Yet the 20 percent of the world's people who live in the high-income countries account for 86 percent of the total private consumption expenditures. In latter years, the gap between the rich and poor has widened enormously.

Though we in Canada are blessed beyond belief by world standards, we have no reason to be smug or complacent. In the past ten years, the number of poor people in Canada has risen from 3.7 million to more than 5 million, which is 18 percent of the population; more than 1.5 million children (one in five of all the children in the country) live in poverty. Across Canada, governments have slashed social, health, and education funding. Government deficits have been reduced on the backs of the poor. Canada's aid program has been emasculated, but the country's military spending stays at excessively high levels.

Gross disparities and misplaced priorities at home and abroad are staring us in the face. Social justice in a world of plenty seems farther off than ever. The double standards of politics reveal an intellectual corruption aided and abetted by a corporate-controlled media. There is an anger inside me as I see what exists and what ought to be.

We fight wars that should not be fought. We maintain nuclear weapons that constantly endanger humanity. We spend money on excessive militarism at the expense of the poor. The way in which the public is manipulated into believing that militarism buys peace is the greatest intellectual insult of all.

Fulminating against outrage is not very productive. Anger without correction merely leads to cynicism. I have tried throughout my professional life to point to new and better ways to attain peace and human security. Lighting a candle rather than cursing the darkness has been far more satisfying. And I have learned along the way.

One of the things I learned was not to close doors of opportunity. While it was not very appealing to immerse myself once more in the slings and arrows of public life, nor to get on an airplane every week to fly to Ottawa and live in a hotel, I realized that a senatorial base would give me access to more decision-makers and enlarge my ability to be heard.

I was still running a mixture of emotions—astonishment, apprehension, pleasure—when Prime Minister Jean Chretien called me a few days later. He said he wanted to recognize the work I had done on peace issues and encouraged me to use the Senate platform to widen my audience on the United Nations' issues of disarmament, development, and human rights. When he then said I could sit as an Independent Senator, I realized in a flash that the maximum moment in my life had come: I could use my experience, knowledge, access, and freedom to tell Canadians what I believe needs to be said about making our society a more humane place. The invitation to join the Senate was an offer I could not refuse.

My re-immersion into the political world came through a controversial appointment. The movement for an elected Senate had been building up in Alberta for some time, the result of a feeling of political alienation. An election was actually under way in Alberta in which voters in municipal elections could also designate Senators in Waiting. The Prime Minister did not recognize such an ad hoc election, which is not provided for in the Constitution of Canada. The Constitution provides for the Governor General, upon the advice of the Prime Minister, to summon qualified persons to the Senate. The Prime Minister, to uphold his constitutional position, had decided to make an appointment in the same manner that all 105 Canadian Senators have been appointed. And he was selecting me.

The Reform Party leadership criticized the manner of the appointment but did not attack me personally. Actually, I felt a great deal of support throughout the province.

With many other politicians and people across Canada, I believe in an elected Senate and am working to bring this about through a due process of constitutional reform. The Senate certainly needs to be reformed. It should be elected, more equitable in its representation, and more effective. That struggle continues, as we expand democracy in the modern world. But I did not become a Senator to work only on this one political problem. Political machinations are always with us.

In my first speech to the Senate, I presented three issues that are central to me personally—equitable economic and social development, reform of the Senate, and setting out a forthright Canadian policy to support the abolition of nuclear weapons. I talked about the poverty I had seen in Alberta and called for a re-investment, now that Alberta's economy was flourishing, in the essential social programs that have been so severely affected by the province's cutbacks. I drew the attention of the Senate to the "high potential for a significant Canadian contribution to international peace and security" and called upon Canada "to work for peace, reconciliation and social justice in the world."

It is the social justice agenda that I want to devote the major share of my energies to. There is too much suffering, too many disparities, too much political duplicity, too much danger in the world for me to be silent. The outrages of militarism and poverty must be addressed. To advance a political agenda for social justice is the reason I became an Alberta Senator.

Bread Not Bombs is about a peace for the 21st century that can only be obtained by advancing a social justice agenda. My theme throughout is that in the new world of "globalization," peace, security, and development are inter-linked and must be advanced simultaneously through an integrated agenda. The crises in the world, which I elaborate in the first part, "Human Insecurity: Double Standards," are so severe that urgent political attention is required. Building the conditions for peace, described in the second part, "Human Security: An Agenda for the 21st Century," is the new "reality" of our time. The new tools of public diplomacy, outlined in the final part, "Social Justice: A Daily Struggle," must be used. The agenda I describe can no longer be dismissed as "idealistic." The multiple crises in the world demand a higher form of politics.

Human Insecurity
Double Standards

Bread Not Bombs

The Poor
Get Poorer

1

Quite simply, poverty is growing dramatically in Alberta. This poverty is not only among social assistance recipients and the marginally employed. Poverty is also growing among working families and among previously middle class families.

...

Cuts to social assistance payments have placed recipients not just below the "poverty line" (which they were before), but below the "basic necessities line." These Albertans cannot meet basic requirements for life like food and shelter anymore.

Listen To Me, Report of the Quality of Life Commission

In the mid-1990s, I was asked to join the Quality of Life Commission, formed by a group of citizens in Edmonton concerned about the effect of the Alberta Government's social spending cuts on the lives of poor people. My eyes were opened to the plight of the poor in Alberta. The Commission, operating with modest means, exposed the human dimensions of the poverty scandal in Canada. That scandal lies not only in the fact that governments are letting the poor get poorer but that they are being marginalized in a society increasingly dominated by the strong and rich.

After many interviews with poor people in Alberta, the Commission produced a report, *Listen to Me*. It recorded the stories of several Albertans, mostly women, minorities, aboriginal people, and children, whose quality of life had deteriorated as a result of government cuts in education, health, and social services. Those cuts were instituted when Premier Ralph Klein was elected in 1993 and the new government determined to wipe out the $3.8 billion deficit. This was accomplished in two years through such measures as a 20 percent cut in every department's budget. Health services were restricted, social assistance payments cut drastically, and tuition at post-secondary institutions hiked sharply.

A well-educated mother of three children living on social assistance told the Commission that she had recently developed a small business that needed a few months to reach the point where she would no longer need social assistance. The social services department ruled that if she continued her business she would no longer be eligible for social assistance. Fearful that she would not be able to provide for her children over the next few months, she dropped the business to ensure her eligibility. "With a little flexibility, I could be on my own now," she said. "Instead, I'm still on welfare."

An inner city minister operating a food bank said that before the government cuts, his church gave out food to 400 persons a month; in two years the number jumped to 3,000. The church used to serve a hot meal once a week to about 250 people; after the cuts, the hot meal was provided daily. A clothing bank used to be open one day a week; with increased demand, it began to operate daily and spread to a whole floor of the church.

A young single mother finishing her fourth year of university told the Commission that when she graduated, her student loan would be "enormous." She said: "I would like not to have to worry about how I'm going to clothe my children and provide for them. I would like not to have to worry about running out of toilet paper and female hygiene products. I would like to know that I can go to the hospital and receive service for health needs."

The object of the government cutbacks was not only to eliminate the annual deficit but to pay down the debt. The deficit was quickly curbed and, by 1999, the province's net debt was eliminated (meaning the province's assets exceeded existing debt). The government celebrated this accomplishment 11 years ahead of schedule by giving a free hot dog lunch to government employees. Lost in the celebration was the price the poor had paid through shrinking municipal grants, low welfare support, hospital bed closures, soaring tuition fees and large class sizes, and reduced services for the mentally disabled.

After the initial severe cutbacks, the government did increase its funding in the health, education, and social services sectors, but when population growth and inflation are factored in, all three areas continue to suffer from under-funding. Stories abound of the continued heavy demand on food banks, the dramatic increase in child welfare caseloads, the doubling of university tuition costs in a five-year period, and the overloaded conditions in the province's hospitals. While funding for public programs had at one time been among the highest in the country, Alberta ranks last among the provinces in per capita public health expenditures.

In addition to the financial cutbacks, a harshness towards the poor began to be noted, as elitist private interests not only captured the public policy agenda but public debate as well. When the Quality of Life Commission brought its findings to a meeting with four government ministers, the politicians dismissed our report as "anecdotal." We tried to point out that inordinate financial pressures on the poor creates an alienated class that destabilizes society.

Poverty, family breakdown, and alienation come with consequences. People are left fragile, isolated, and apathetic. The negative effects of such social exclusion are resentment and disaffection, and they ultimately erode the threads of social fabric. Families who do not get proper nutrition are sick more often. This costs more in health services. Families who experience long-term unemployment are more likely to break down, causing more poverty and isolation. Alienation increases the risk of addiction, which has a high human cost and a high financial cost in health services and addiction counseling. Young people who come from troubled families are more likely to fall into crime. This costs society through the justice and penal systems. We invited the government to undertake its own comprehensive, province-wide investigation, similar to what the Quality of Life Commission had done, to find out for itself the effects of the growing rich-poor gap. The recommendation went unheeded.

Just as I was entering the Senate in 1998, the Edmonton Social Planning Council issued a report, stating that the number of families in Edmonton living in absolute poverty had increased from 3.3 percent in 1993 to 8.1 percent in 1995. It is very difficult to define absolute poverty, but it generally means an inability to access the basic amounts of food, shelter, clothing, and other necessities for survival. For single-parent families in Edmonton, the rate of absolute poverty increased from 17.1 percent to 24.8 percent, the highest rate among Canadian cities.

It was becoming clear to me that the social safety net, which has always been so fundamental to our Canadian sense of fair play and justice, was breaking down, not just in Alberta but across Canada. Despite their imperfections, social programs have kept thousands of Canadians from falling too far out of the social and economic mainstream; today the increasing numbers of children growing up in poverty may be set so far back they will never recover.

I took this concern to the Senate. In my maiden speech, I praised the government of Alberta for developing the fastest-growing economy in Canada and for balancing the budget and significantly reducing the province's debt. But fiscal management had come at a cost. Cuts in health, education, and social spending have had a deleterious effect on our society and particularly on the most vulnerable people, those in low-paying jobs, the aged, the ill, children, and single parents. "We have allowed our social programs to be dismantled by those who see poverty as an individual failing, instead of the more complicated problem it is," I said. "Now that our fiscal accounts are in order, and on behalf of the disadvantaged in our society, I call for a restoration of health and education spending as an investment in the continued development of our people." I added that the responsibility for this rests on both the federal and provincial governments, and an adequate federal-provincial funding formula based on national standards is required.

Premier Klein's reaction was immediate and defensive, criticizing me for my view of the effect of the cuts in health, education, and welfare. He pointed out that the Alberta government was not dismantling its social programs and that, in fact, health and education funding were increasing, and that the Alberta Family Employment Tax Credit in 1998 provided $75 million to 160,000 low- to middle-income working families with children. Two of Premier Klein's ministers, Dr. Lyle Oberg, Minister of Family and Social Services, and Halvar Jonson, Minister of Health, wrote me similar letters of protest. Neither minister referred to the findings of the Alberta Medical Association, which showed that 81.9 percent of the 10,000 Albertans who responded to a survey said that they or a family member had been forced to wait for health care at some time during the past 12 months; 58.3 percent said the wait created extra stress on their families.

A few months after my speech, the Parkland Institute, a research organization located on the campus of the University of Alberta, held a public policy forum, "Poverty Amidst Plenty," on growing poverty and disparity in Alberta. The keynote speaker was Armine Yalnizyan, author of *The Growing Gap: A Report on Growing Inequality Between the Rich and Poor in Canada*, published by the Centre for Social Justice, Toronto. Yalnizyan told the forum that while Alberta's economy is growing rapidly, the gap between rich and poor is expanding more rapidly than anywhere else in Canada. The middle class is shrinking as more people slip into low-income groups. "Alberta, as a province, is leading the bandwagon in terms of deteriorating equality of income, though it is one of the economic engines of the country," she said. The *Edmonton Journal* headlined its report: "Albertans Ignore Plight of Poor—Economist."

Premier Klein responded to the story by attacking the Parkland Institute in a letter to Rod Fraser, President of the University of Alberta, stating "I am dismayed to see yet another one-sided and ideologically biased attack on the generosity of Albertans by the factually challenged Parkland Institute." Fraser issued a statement saying he would take no action against Parkland, despite Klein's thinly veiled attempt at intimidation. Then, former Premier Don Getty, also a Conservative, weighed into the debate, asserting that the Klein government, which had succeeded Getty's government, had "blundered badly on health and education."

The debate over widening social inequality in Alberta has entered a new stage with the government's plans for a flat tax. A flat tax is little more than a thinly disguised tax break for upper income Albertans. Lower income earners will get a small tax break, but the revenues needed to sustain single tier, high quality public education and health care will be reduced. As such services are starved of funds, the well-to-do will abandon them for private sector services, leaving lower-income earners to rely on lower quality public services. High quality public services are the great equalizer, and what is saved in this flat tax will only impair the ability of governments to finance programs to alleviate poverty.

In their protests against criticism, Premier Klein and his ministers have shown themselves to be very sensitive to any allegations or suggestions that they are uncaring towards the poor. They may be in denial about the effects of their policies on the most vulnerable, they may trumpet their good deeds, but down deep they appear to recognize that it is still a political liability in Canada to be seen to be hurting the poor. That is at least a sign of hope that the political system will not, in the end, be impervious to the cries of the poor.

Poverty Is a National Disgrace

The 1990s proved to be a shameful record of governmental disregard of the poor across Canada.

- In 1996, 17.9 percent or 5.3 million Canadians were below the poverty line; 60.8 percent of single mothers live in poverty; 20.8 percent of seniors live in poverty (an increase of 11 percent in a three-year period); 44 percent of the Aboriginal population off-reserve live in poverty.

- Ten years after the House of Commons unanimously passed a resolution in 1989 to eliminate poverty among Canadian children by 2000, one in five children in Canada lives in poverty. This is an increase of 564,000 children since 1989.

- The use of food banks across Canada doubled from 1989 to 1997; 75 percent of the 162,000 people who received food from the food banks in 1998 were on welfare.

- There are more than 200,000 homeless in Canada.

- In 1973, the richest 10 percent of families with children under 18 made 21 times more than the poorest 10 percent of Canadian families. In 1996, the richest 10 percent of families made 314 times more than the poorest 10 percent of Canadian families.

- In 1973, 60 percent of families earned between $24,500 and $65,000 (in 1996 dollars). By 1996, that middle class shrunk: only 44 percent of families with dependent children made between $24,500 and $65,000.

- Welfare rates, welfare eligibility, and/or shelter allowances have been reduced in almost every province since 1995.

So incensed was the National Anti-Poverty Organization (NAPO) that growing numbers of Canadians were being denied basic human rights, it took the unprecedented step in 1998 of bringing their protests against the callous attitude of governments in Canada to the United Nations Committee on Economic, Social and Cultural Rights in Geneva. NAPO excoriated federal and provincial governments for allowing the social safety net to collapse. "Due in large part to extreme measures by both federal and provincial governments in the name of debt and deficit reduction, the past five years have seen the most dramatic reversal of social and economic equalization initiatives since Canada's social security system was set up over 30 years ago."

It was ironic that the Canadian government should be called before a U.N. Committee to explain why there is so much poverty in Canada since, for the past five years, Canada has been ranked at the top of the U.N.'s Human Development Index. The government takes pleasure in regularly proclaiming that the U.N. rates Canada as the best country in the world by quality of life standards. In its defence, the government told the Committee that continued increases in government spending in the 1970s and 1980s, on social programs in particular, led to rising deficits and a large debt in the 1980s and 1990s. The 1990s thus saw reductions in social expenditures in the face of the serious debt situation; however, funding was being increased for welfare programs.

The U.N. Committee did not accept this explanation, bluntly telling Canada to get its priorities straight. "The Canadian government beat the deficit, but they did so at the expense of a high poverty rate in Canada," said the Egyptian representative, Mahmoud Samir Ahmed. Committee members expressed frustration that their efforts to get answers on the extent of homelessness, the lack of subsidized housing, and the levels of poverty among single women were stymied by vague answers.

Nonetheless, the Committee was able to find out enough to criticize Canada severely.

The Committee is gravely concerned that such a wealthy country as Canada has allowed the problem of homelessness and inadequate housing to grow to such proportions that the mayors of Canada's ten largest cities have now declared homelessness a national disaster.

The Committee is concerned that provincial social assistance rates and other income assistance measures have clearly not been adequate to cover the rental costs of the poor. In the last five years, the number of tenants paying more than 50% of income toward rent has increased by 43%.

The Committee is also concerned about the inadequate legal protection in Canada of women's rights.

The Committee is greatly concerned at the gross disparity between Aboriginal people and the majority of Canadians... There has been little or no progress in the alleviation of social and economic deprivation among Aboriginal people. In particular, the Committee is deeply concerned at the shortage of adequate housing, the endemic mass unemployment and the high rate of suicide, especially among youth in the Aboriginal communities.

The Committee is deeply concerned to receive information that provincial courts in Canada have routinely opted for an interpretation which excludes protection of the right to an adequate standard of living and other covenant rights.

This indictment is nothing short of a national disgrace. Why are we tolerating it?

In 1976, Canada signed the International Covenant of Economic, Social and Cultural Rights, which affirmed the right of everyone to an adequate standard of living, including food, clothing and shelter, the right of everyone to work, to enjoy the highest attainable physical and mental health, and the right to education. Many Canadians enjoy a high standard of living and quality of life. We used to pride ourselves that those suffering economic hardship were protected by a social safety net. This net was held together by the Canadian Assistance Plan (CAP), under which the federal government provided 50 percent of the funding of welfare and social services to the provinces. In return, the provinces were required to provide assistance based on need and at adequate levels. In 1990, as Canada entered a recession, the federal government limited its contributions under the CAP to increases of 5 percent per year for Ontario, British Columbia, and Alberta. By 1993, instead of cost sharing 50–50, it was paying only 28 percent of welfare costs in Ontario.

Having eroded the CAP, the federal government unilaterally eliminated it in 1996, and replaced it with the Canada Health and Social Transfer, which puts funding for social assistance, health, and post-secondary education all in the same pool. There are no conditions on how this money is to be used. The only national standard for welfare retained is the right not to be discriminated against because of residency. The door has been opened for the gutting of social assistance systems across Canada.

This situation is compounded by the cuts in the Employment Insurance (EI) program. Many workers and their families who previously would have been covered by EI during times of unemployment have been forced to turn to social assistance. There has been an astounding decrease in the proportion of unemployed Canadians covered by EI. According to a recent Canadian Labour Congress report, fewer than 25 percent of the unemployed in Ontario are eligible for EI.

Thus, tightened social benefits cut the federal government's expenditures so drastically that, like Alberta, it quickly achieved a balanced budget. The fiscal deficit was gone, and the poor paid the price, but what of the social deficit? Seeing deficits melting away, the rich and strong across Canada began clamouring for tax cuts or ploughing new surpluses into debt reduction. The call to re-institute social programs to protect the increasingly vulnerable people who cannot keep up with a new technologically driven society has been muted. Not many in government are listening to the poor.

Moreover, the idea has taken hold that governments are unable to cope with the new financial forces of globalization. The markets, not governments, occupy the commanding heights of economic development. But the market has no accountability and is unconcerned with the common fate of society, relying instead upon competing individual private interests who are then increasingly more powerful and coercive than government. The idea of equality is overshadowed by a system devoted to a pursuit of profit that views political and social regulation and responsibility as constraints to be discouraged as well as opposed.

The social contract of key social rights—long a hallmark of Canadian society—eroded under pressure from the ideology of the 1990s. That ideology, whether called neo-conservatism or neo-liberalism, proclaimed that governments should get out of the way, markets would lift the economy with corporate tax breaks, and the poor would benefit from "trickle down" wealth. This ideology undermines the ethical and moral foundation upon which society is built by propagating the irrelevance of social investment.

The ominous trend here is the implicit removal of responsibility and accountability of economic decisions from a society in which the impact of unregulated markets are demanding huge sacrifices and exacting profound social costs. What we have actually seen is a surge in wealth of those at the top of the economic ladder with increasing numbers left out of the new march to progress. The "caring and sharing" society that Canada used to be is gone. Those who advocate social justice as a basis for the formulation of public policy are relegated to the sidelines of public discussion.

Aid Cut to World's Poor

When we look at the world scene, which is even more unjust than the plight of the poor in Alberta and Canada, the cries of the poor should have the loudness of thunder, but they too are seldom heard. The vast disparities between rich and poor, a growing concern in Canada, is a constant refrain in the developing countries of the South. And it is in the South where the great majority of world population growth—from 6 billion today to 8.5 billion in 2025—is taking place.

Of the 4.4 billion peoples in developing countries, nearly three-fifths lack basic sanitation. A third has no access to clean water. A quarter does not have adequate housing. A fifth has no access to modern health services. A fifth of children do not attend school beyond grade five. Another fifth do not have enough dietary energy and protein.

In 34 developing countries, including Jordan, Malaysia, Russia, Peru, South Africa, Ukraine, Venezuela, and Zambia, the richest 20 percent of the population receives more than half the country's income, while the poorest 20 percent get less than 5 percent.

These figures often seem abstract and remote. But I do not see them that way. I see them in the faces of the poor I have met in many journeys through developing countries. The children outside the mosque in Bangladesh who started a near-riot when I gave a couple of them some pennies taught me what poverty does to children. The emaciated woman who thrust a naked baby in my arms revealed a desperation that numbers cannot convey.

Yet numbers as well as faces tell us what is happening in the world. In 1960, the richest 20 percent of people in the

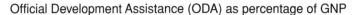

Official Development Assistance (ODA) as percentage of GNP

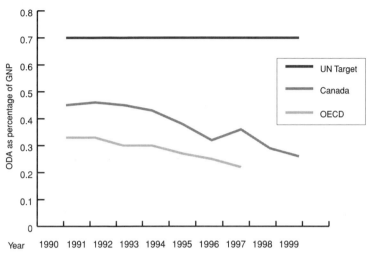

Source: Judith Randel and Tony German, eds., Eurostep ICVA, *The Reality of Aid 1997/1998: An Independent Review of Development Cooperation* (London: Earthscan Publications Ltd., 1997); Canadian Council for International Cooperation (1998–99 figures).

world had an income 30 times greater than the poorest fifth; by 1990 the richest 20 percent had an income 60 times greater than the poorest fifth. The richest fifth in the world consume 58 percent of total energy, while the poorest fifth make do on less than 4 percent.

While living standards have catapulted ahead for the industrialized countries in the last half of the 20th century, the poorest have been further marginalized. Conference after conference has been called by the U.N. Analyses, strategies, and plans galore have been publicized, debated, and promised. But when it comes to putting money into development programs, government priorities are elsewhere. When the Earth Summit in Rio was held in 1992, the 600-page Agenda 21 was adopted to deal with the myriad problems standing in the way of sustainable development. The North, asked to come up with $125 billion as its share of the $625 billion plan, pledged a paltry $2 billion.

Official Development Assistance (ODA), the aid provided by the 21 industrialized countries in the Organization for Economic Cooperation and Development (OECD) to the developing countries, has declined continually since the Earth Summit. The seven richest countries in the world have imposed the steepest cuts in their aid programs. Cuts in aid have hit hardest the countries with the most pressing human needs, including those with high child death rates, high birth rates, and low access to safe drinking water. In 1999, the Red Cross reported that in the past six years 25 million people had been driven from their homes by drought, flooding, deforestation, and soil problems; shantytowns have multiplied throughout developing countries.

The pledge by rich countries to provide every child on earth with a basic level of literacy by 2015 has been abandoned. Very little is now heard of the U.N. target established in 1969 of 0.7 percent of GNP to be devoted to ODA. Only four countries, Sweden, Norway, Denmark, and the Netherlands have achieved the 0.7 percent target. In 1997, the United States was at 0.09 percent, the U.K. at 0.26 percent, and Canada at 0.34 percent.

Though private investment has enabled growth to take place in the strongest of the developing nations, private investment seeks an immediate return. There is no immediate return on investing in the health, education, and social underpinning of a people. It takes years for such investment to be rewarded in the greater health and education of a people. That is why Official Development Assistance is needed. Yet ODA is dominated by the economic interests of the donor country, seeking jobs at home to make the goods shipped abroad in the name of aid. Only a small part of ODA actually reaches the poorest, but even this pittance has shown spectacular results in uplifting the lives of the most vulnerable.

The debt overhang of developing countries, exceeding $1.3 trillion, cripples their development and forces even more cutbacks in health and education services, as foreign debt servicing swallows up public revenues. Debt forgiveness programs have been talked about but rarely implemented. The burden on the poorest gets heavier, and inequality widens as they suffer further marginalization and disempowerment.

There is yet another factor–militarism–evident in the misplaced priorities of governments and impacting adversely on the poor of the world. Militarism, which remains a dominant characteristic of the world despite what many thought to be the end of the Cold War, has unseen consequences that need to be exposed to a public spotlight.

The Cold War Is **Not Over** 2

The 1990s started out being called the "post-Cold War era." The Berlin Wall had fallen, democracy raced through Eastern Europe, the Soviet Union dissolved. There was even talk, briefly, of a "New World Order."

Then Iraq invaded Kuwait and the Gulf War followed. Wars also broke out in the African States of Somalia, Rwanda, and Sierra Leone. The dismembering of Yugoslavia produced unprecedented slaughters in Bosnia and Kosovo. A total of 103 armed conflicts in the 1990s led to the deaths of more than five million people and the displacement of one in every 200 people in the world. Forty-two of these conflicts qualified as wars because more than 1,000 people were killed in each one. So much for a new world order.

Genocide in Rwanda, Bosnia, and Kosovo have at least received worldwide publicity. But other wars, hardly less murderous, have been almost completely ignored. Wars in the 1990s in Congo-Brazzaville, Angola, Ethiopia and Eritrea, Sierra Leone, Liberia, and the Sudan have claimed several million lives. In Africa as a whole, there are now some four million refugees and probably at least ten million internally displaced persons.

Africa has the largest share of conflict today. But no part of the world is immune. At the end of the 20th century, the scourge of war returned, with a vengeance, to Europe, the continent which produced the two world wars in the first half of the century.

As civilization has surged ahead, acts of barbarism have sunk to new depravities. Wholesale exterminations, genocide, mass killings, deportations, tortures in the extreme have forever scarred the memory of a century that, ironically, saw one scientific invention after another to prolong and enhance life. When the century started, wars took only one civilian life for every nine military combatants killed. Now it is the reverse: nine civilians are killed for every soldier and, most shockingly, 80 percent of war deaths are women and children.

The tragedy of the Serbian expulsion of the Albanians from Kosovo shows once again that distinctions between combatants and civilians disappear in battles fought from village to village and street to street. Any and all tactics of violence are employed, from systematic rape to scorched-earth tactics that destroy crops and poison wells, to ethnic cleansing and genocide. With the standards of common decency abandoned, human rights violations against children and women occur in unprecedented numbers.

In the past decade, two million children have been killed in armed conflicts; four to five million more have been disabled and more than twelve million made homeless. Many more millions have been traumatized by the atrocities they have been forced to witness or take part in. Still other children suffer the effects of sexual violence or the multiple deprivations of armed conflict that expose them to hunger or disease. Child soldiers were a common sight in the wars in Afghanistan, Iran, Iraq, and Mozambique.

These facts are shocking enough, but more chilling is the conclusion to be drawn from them: more and more of the world is being sucked into a desolate moral vacuum. This is a space devoid of the most basic human values; a space in which children are slaughtered, raped, and maimed; they are starved and exposed to extreme brutality; they are exploited as soldiers; still others are forced into child labour. Such unregulated terror and violence speak of deliberate victimization. Nelson Mandela's wife, Graça Machel, studied this situation on behalf of the U.N. and concluded: "There are few further depths to which humanity can sink."

If governments and societies tolerate such bestiality, then it must be stopped by United Nations enforcement, an action that requires first of all strengthening the U.N.

The dawning of the new Millennium has illuminated an array of hopes that, finally, the human race will be able to put human butcheries behind us. Biology tells us that we are not genetically programmed to violence. What, then, is stopping us from building the conditions for global peace?

The usual suspects—greed, power, selfishness, apathy— suggest themselves as the source of conflict. Doubtless, they all feed the fires of war. But the greatest obstacle we face is the unwillingness of the political systems of the world to build a system of enforceable world law.

The record of 20th century wars shows how desperately we need a legal and international authority, not only to stop fighting, but to root out the seeds of conflict as well. Modern wars do not just happen. They spring from the terrible disparities in the possession of wealth and resources, from the bursting of an oppressed people seeking self-determination, from racial hatreds, and cultural hostilities. Wars are fought by the use of weapons that are, in many cases, supplied to combatants by arms merchants easily able to escape the weak government strictures imposed against the arms trade.

The hot and cold wars of the 20th century were mainly fought over the great ideological divides: Democracy against Nazism; Capitalism versus Communism; self-determination versus imperialism. But the armed conflicts of the 1990s have been fought over the access to natural resources and the inability of weak States to mediate between the competing demands of various internal ethnic, racial, and religious groups. These conflicts have largely dealt with disputes *within* States over land ownership, environmental change, water scarcity, and food shortages, and illustrate the link between armed conflict and social and economic development.

For example, the Chiapas rebellion in Mexico, the guerrilla movements in Colombia, and conflicts in Senegal and Mauritania were based on opposition movements' claims to large land tracts held by rich landowners. In the Sahel region of Africa, environmental damage, particularly desertification, has caused conflict in Mali, Niger, and Chad. Disputes in the Middle East in Israel, Lebanon, Syria, and Jordan have been linked to water, particularly to the Jordan River. Riots in Indonesia and Lesotho stemmed from the sudden rise in the price of food. Food supplies were deliberately disrupted in wars in Mozambique, Angola, Somalia, and the Sudan, resulting in mass starvation.

Building peace and prosperity requires greater attention to the role of equitable access to and distribution of resources, particularly agriculture, in breaking the vicious cycle of violent conflict and scarcity in low-income countries. However, in the 1990s, wealthy States cut back on aid, installed protectionist measures against imports from poor countries, and failed to provide adequate relief to war-torn societies.

The opportunity costs of continued armed conflict are alarming. The United Nations Development Program reports that conflicts destroy years of progress in building social infrastructure, establishing functioning government institutions, fostering community-level solidarity and social cohesion, and promoting economic development.

Like war itself, sustainable peace does not just happen. It requires the continued cultivation of economic and social development. It does not seem to have occurred to political leaders that the fight against hunger, scarcity, environmental pollution, and poverty can also convert hapless soldiers of violence into productive members of the global community.

Hypocrisies and the Arms Trade

The traffic in arms reveals the blatant hypocrisy of the five major powers in the world: the United States, Russia, the United Kingdom, France, and China. These five are the permanent members of the U.N. Security Council, the declared Nuclear Weapons States, and the biggest exporters of arms. It is incredible that the very States charged with maintaining peace and security in the world are at the same time the proliferators of weaponry from small arms to intercontinental missiles.

No wonder there are wars, increasingly characterized by societies torn apart by endemic violence, when arms are so easily obtainable. Since 1960, the global arms trade amounted to at least $1.5 trillion. Two-thirds of that went to developing countries—often indebting the recipients and skewing their national budget priorities in the process. From 1984 to 1995, the developing world received 15,000 tanks, 34,000 artillery pieces, 27,000 armoured personnel carriers and armoured cars, 1,000 warships and submarines, 4,200 combat aircraft, 3,000 helicopters, 48,000 missiles, and millions of small-calibre arms.

While the current global arms trade of $25 billion a year is less than the peak years of the Cold War, it is an increase over the earlier years of the 1990s. The U.S. is the dominant exporter, having increased its share of deliveries to 43 percent. The major recipients of arms continue to be the countries of Asia and the Middle East, where cauldrons are continually brewing.

This massive infusion of arms further destabilized countries and regions that were in the throes of anti-colonial struggles, ethnic battles, and numerous other unresolved conflicts. States have put great energy and enormous resources into developing ever more sophisticated and destructive weapons, in the process relentlessly building up toward ever-higher levels of organized violence.

It is often said that guns do not cause wars, people do. But it cannot be denied that the illicit accumulation of such weapons has acted as a catalyst for many of the world's most chronic conflicts. Weapons and ammunition are readily available at cheap prices from multiple sources. The international arms trade has made assault rifles cheap and widely available so the poorest communities now have access to deadly weapons capable of transforming any local conflict into a bloody slaughter. In Uganda, an AK-47 automatic machine gun can be purchased for the price of a chicken and, in Northern Kenya, it can be bought for the price of a goat. Previously, the more dangerous weapons were either heavy or complex, but newer guns are so light that children can use them and so simple that they can be stripped and reassembled by a child of ten. The proliferation of inexpensive light weapons has resulted in more children becoming "soldiers."

Light weapons, constantly improved for accuracy, mobility, and ease of concealment, are finding their way not just to more countries but to more private arsenals within those countries, including militia groups, drug cartels, and organized crime syndicates, creating an insidious and pervasive "gun culture." The manufacturers, distributors, and even original buyers of these weapons often do not know who will ultimately use them.

Some steps are being taken throughout the international community to curb this traffic in the tools of violence. The U.N. maintains a voluntary register of mid-sized armaments (but not light arms). Humanitarian efforts are mounted to deal with casualties. Yet there is no international legal system to prevent the global arms trade.

Just as nothing is being done to stop the trade in arms, the world community seems powerless to check military expenditures of all kinds. The world's annual expenditures of nearly $800 billion on defence are about 600 times larger than the annual core budget of the United Nations.

The United States alone spends more than $280 billion on maintaining its military might. This dwarfs the spending of any other nation. All the other NATO countries plus Japan and South Korea spend $202 billion; Russia, the nation with the

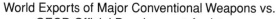

World Exports of Major Conventional Weapons vs. OECD Official Development Assistance

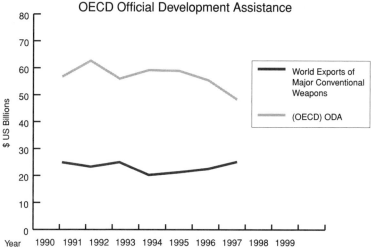

Note: These figures are based on the addition of 32 countries with aggregate 1993–1997 exports of less than $100 million to the 30 leading suppliers of major conventional weapons for 1993–1997.

Source: *SIPRI Yearbook 1998: Armaments, Disarmament, and International Security* (Oxford: Oxford University Press, 1998).

second largest military budget, spends $64 billion; China $37 billion. Those States the U.S. labels as "rogues," Cuba, Iraq, Iran, Libya, North Korea, the Sudan, and Syria together spend only a total of $16 billion.

Yet the Clinton Administration has decreed that its military spending is not high enough and plans additional spending of $12 billion over the next six years. This plan was set even before the Kosovo war, which consumed so much ammunition that Pentagon planners worried they would run out of bombs before new ones could be produced. The budget for the year 2000 alone includes a $43 billion jump in procurement of new weapons, an increase of 8.1 percent. The Pentagon continues to invest billions in Cold War systems from the FIA-18E/F Fighter to Tomahawk Cruise Missiles to destroyers and landing ships. Even these new systems are not enough. The U.S. military research-and-development budget is more than seven times that of France, its nearest competitor. In recent years, the U.S. share of world military spending rose from 30 percent to 34 percent and is still increasing.

Nuclear Weapons: For None or All

Astounding as they are, these figures pale beside what the U.S. and the other nuclear weapons powers spend on nuclear weapons. The United States spends $100 million *each day* on maintaining and upgrading its arsenal of 15,400 nuclear weapons. Since the nuclear age began in 1945, the nuclear powers have spent $8 trillion on developing, producing, and maintaining their nuclear arsenals; of this total, the U.S. spent $5.5 trillion. It is impossible to calculate how much of the world's developmental needs could have been met with such sums. While the Cold War has been blamed for the nuclear arms races, there is no reason today to justify the retention of nuclear weapons. They have not only outlandish economic costs but political and social consequences making the world a more dangerous place than even existed during the Cold War.

When India and Pakistan successfully tested nuclear weapons in 1998, thus becoming de facto members of the nuclear club, many governments expressed shock. It reminded me of the police officer in the film *Casablanca* who, upon being handed his winnings following a police raid on a gambling den he was supposed to have been supervising, exclaimed he was "shocked" to find out gambling had been going on. India and Pakistan, along with Israel, long ago began developing a nuclear weapons capacity. It should have been no surprise to anyone that India and Pakistan took overt action to prove that they are major powers too.

In the 1960s, when fears grew that nuclear weapons might spread to several countries, a bargain was made between the "Nuclear Weapons States" (NWS) and the "Non-Nuclear Weapons States" (NNWS). The bargain took the form of the

Non-Proliferation Treaty (NPT) in which the NWS agreed to negotiate nuclear disarmament if the NNWS would agree not to acquire nuclear weapons. When the NPT came into force in 1970, there were 38,526 nuclear weapons in existence; not only was the number not reduced, by the peak of the Cold War in the 1980s, the number jumped to 69,490. By 1995, when the NPT was indefinitely extended, there were still more nuclear weapons in existence than in 1970. Now there are about 35,000, the great majority of which are held by Russia and the United States.

In the heady days following the fall of the Berlin Wall, Russia and the U.S. bilaterally negotiated reductions. START I (the first Strategic Arms Reduction Talks) was ratified and implemented; START II was signed and ratified by the U.S. There the progress stopped. The Russian Duma held up START II for several years as, in a weakened military state, Russia became more resentful and fearful of NATO's expansion into three Central European countries, Poland, Hungary and the Czech Republic. Russian generals said they would have to rely on their nuclear weapons, so weak had they become in conventional arms. This stiffened the U.S. Administration's decision to retain nuclear weapons as a hedge against an uncertain future and maintain nuclear deterrence at the core of their military doctrine.

Nuclear disarmament is at a standstill. Even if START II were to be fully implemented, the world would be left in 2007 with 17,000 nuclear weapons of all kinds. That is not the nuclear disarmament that States promised when they signed the NPT.

Anyone who has been to Hiroshima and Nagasaki, as I have, and has seen the awful calamity that beset both cities when they suffered the effects of an atomic bomb in August, 1945, can only be aghast at the spectre of a nuclear fireball. At their peak number, nuclear weapons contained an explosive yield of 18 billion tons of TNT (3.6 tons for every human being), compared with the 6 million tons of explosive force used in all of World War II. New generations must understand what nuclear weapons do. They are not just an advanced form of weaponry; with their radioactive fallout, they have the power to decimate the natural environment that has sustained humanity since the beginning of time.

Former President of the International Court of Justice Mohammed Bedjaoui has called nuclear weapons "the ultimate evil." One would think that sane political leaders would work to rid the world of such instruments—especially now that the Cold War has been proclaimed to be over. But no, it is quite the reverse. The five declared nuclear powers have all stated that nuclear weapons are necessary to their security. NATO (possessing the three Western NWS) calls nuclear weapons "essential." India and Pakistan, noting this, have taken the position that if nuclear weapons are necessary for the major powers, and that, in fact, they define their powers as permanent members of the Security Council through possession of nuclear weapons, then India and Pakistan must have them too. India has been particularly vocal in protesting the discriminatory aspects of the NPT, which it claims permits the NWS to retain their nuclear weapons while proscribing their acquisition by any other state. Actually, the NPT does not give this permission. Article VI of the NPT obliges States to negotiate nuclear disarmament, but it is ignored by the NWS.

The International Court of Justice, in its 1996 ruling on nuclear weapons, said that States were obliged to conclude—not just pursue—such negotiations. But even though it is the highest legal authority in the world, its call has been snubbed by the Western NWS. The Court found that the threat or use of nuclear weapons would contravene all aspects of humanitarian law; but it also said that, in the event of an extreme case of self-defence, it could not rule whether the use of nuclear weapons would be lawful or unlawful. This "escape hatch" was just what the nuclear States needed to bolster their claim that nuclear weapons are just for defence. Accordingly, the NWS have proclaimed that the Court's findings will not alter their nuclear deterrence policies.

However self-serving India's and Pakistan's arguments are, the fact remains that the world faces a choice: either there will be a global ban on all nuclear weapons or they will proliferate into other nations. Iraq, Iran, North Korea, and Libya have all tried to develop nuclear weapons. A world of spreading nuclear weapons will be a nightmare with the possibility of accidents and terrorist use multiplying. Yet the U.S., Russia, the U.K., and France all adamantly refuse to enter a process of comprehensive negotiations. Only China is willing to do so. Thus the NPT is in jeopardy of being eroded in the opening years of the 21st century.

In 1995, the NWS pledged to pursue with determination "systematic and progressive efforts to reduce nuclear weapons globally, with the ultimate goal of eliminating those weapons." Not long after, President Bill Clinton of the U.S. signed Presidential Directive 60, which retained nuclear deterrence as a permanent policy. If the wealthiest, greatest military power on earth must cling to nuclear weapons for security, what possible incentive can any other existing nuclear capable State have for getting rid of its weapons? The U.S. has exacerbated the situation by enshrining in national security policy the intention to field a national ballistic missile defence system. The Pentagon has budgeted $10.5 billion over the next six years to create a workable system. This is a direct challenge to the Anti-Ballistic Missile Treaty, set up by the former Soviet Union and the United States to prevent the establishment of defence systems, which only spur on the development of new offensive arms to elude defences.

Seeing the extraordinary renunciation of the U.S. commitment to negotiate nuclear disarmament under the terms of Article VI of the NPT, a number of NNWS have warned that the NPT may crumble following the 2000 Review. Three preparatory meetings for the 2000 Review, which I attended, revealed the depth of the stalemate between the NWS and the NNWS. Egypt and Indonesia continue to express their outrage. Mexico, incensed at U.S. duplicity, has stated openly that it might withdraw from the Treaty.

What is adding to the ire of many NNWS is not just the noncompliance of the Western NWS with their obligations, but their active campaigning against initiatives to start the disarmament ball rolling. A group of middle-power nations (Brazil, Egypt, Ireland, Mexico, New Zealand, Slovenia, South Africa, and Sweden) formed the New Agenda Coalition (NAC) to press the NWS to move forward. The NAC submitted a resolution to the U.N. General Assembly in 1998 calling upon the NWS "to demonstrate an unequivocal commitment to the speedy and total elimination of their respective nuclear weapons and without delay to pursue in good faith and bring to a conclusion negotiations leading to the elimination of nuclear weapons." Although it was adopted by a vote of 114 nations in favour, 18 opposed, and 38 abstentions, the resolution is inoperable because the nuclear States opposed it. If they had any good faith about eliminating their nuclear weapons, this should have been an easy resolution for the NWS to accept. All it asks is for negotiations to begin—without any time-bound framework as to when they have to conclude.

Not only did they reject the resolution, the three Western NWS campaigned around the world for countries to oppose it and forced Slovenia, a NATO aspirant, to drop out of the New Agenda Coalition. The U.S. sent an emissary to NATO headquarters in Brussels to instruct NATO countries to vote no. The U.S. took the position that the resolution challenges—which it does—the continuation of the military doctrine of nuclear deterrence. Canada let it be known that it would vote yes if one other NATO nation would join it. None would, but when Germany and Canada said they would at least abstain on the vote, ten other NATO countries joined in the abstention, thus sending a resounding signal to the NWS that they wanted to see some movement on nuclear disarmament.

At its 50th Anniversary Summit in 1999, NATO agreed, though grudgingly, to begin a review of its nuclear weapons policies. The review was specifically requested by Canada. So, while NATO's official policy continues to be that nuclear weapons "fulfil an essential role by ensuring uncertainty in the mind of any aggressor about the nature of the Allies' response to military aggression," the Alliance has at least committed itself to reviewing the political value of nuclear weapons. So rigid has been the NWS blockage on nuclear disarmament that this step, small as it is, was seen as a victory in the nuclear disarmament camp.

The maintenance of nuclear weapons is but a reflection of society's willingness to commit violence. It is violence when we sell arms to governments to intimidate, if not wage war against, their neighbours and even their own people. It is violence when great sections of humanity are economically discriminated against and even robbed of their right to basic human needs. Violence is so endemic in our culture that it has become routine. It is certainly violence to threaten to use nuclear weapons against other human beings—against people we do not even know and to place in jeopardy not only their own survival as a people but the natural structure upon which all civilization rests.

The maintenance of nuclear weapons into the 21st century is not to fight wars, although that can never be excluded, but to perpetuate power. This power flows from the structures of greed by which the rich think they have a right to the lion's share of the world's resources, after which they will, in the right mood and setting, share superfluous largesse. The recognition of this essential violence is missing today in public discourse. People have put the ghastly scenes of Hiroshima and Nagasaki out of their minds. "It can't happen again!" However, the likelihood of another Hiroshima is growing, not lessening. As nuclear proliferation spreads, as the NPT is flouted, as rogue regimes and terrorists multiply, as smuggling materials increases, as the desperation of downtrodden people mounts, the chances of another nuclear explosion go up.

Where **Bread** and **Bombs** Intersect

3

One Sunday afternoon a few years ago, I went for a walk in Yaounde, the capital of Cameroon in West Africa. On the outskirts of the city, I came upon a group of about 25 women in colourful boubous, who were wailing. Intrigued, I stood at the back of the crowd watching the ceremony. A man came over to me and introduced himself as the father of a two-year-old boy who had just been buried. He invited me into his home. I tried to resist, expressing my condolences and not wanting to intrude. He insisted.

The man was an official in a government department. His house was made of wood and sparsely furnished. I met his wife and three other children. When I asked him how his little boy had died, he pointed to his middle. "Dysentery?" I asked. Yes. "Where do you get your water?" I asked. He took me down the street to the edge of the community and pointed to a dirty mud creek that women used for their washing and where animals were running in and out of the water. "Children drink that water!" I exclaimed. "Well, actually," the man explained, "there is a pipe up on the hill with clean water, but it only works four hours a day and you have to pay to use it. So the children drink from the creek."

When the father told me that story, he spoke for the millions of parents who bury their children every year because the children succumb to waterborne diseases and malnutrition. Every minute of every day, 27 of the world's children die from lack of clean water, adequate nourishment, and proper health care. Waterborne diseases account for 90 percent of these 13 million child deaths each year. Dysentery is the number one cause of death for children the world over. When assessing the priorities of the world's governments, imagine the positive effects from something so basic as clean drinking water.

UNICEF has warned that the decline of foreign aid in the 1990s has been so sharp and swift that millions of children, even if they survive, will leave the 20th century without the most basic standards of health and education promised by world leaders in 1990. That was the year of the Children's Summit at the United Nations when government leaders promised to lift children out of abject poverty. Since then, the aid total from the world's seven richest nations has been cut by about 30 percent— $15 billion in real terms—in areas with the most pressing human needs, including those with high child death rates, high birth rates, and low access to safe drinking water. The bleak reality is that more than one billion people, the overwhelming majority of which are among the world's poor, do not have access to a guaranteed supply of water.

Nations have also broken their promise of education for all children. Across the world, 125 million primary school-aged children will not attend class this year. Another 150 million will drop out without basic literacy skills. The cycle of poverty and illiteracy remains intact for countless children.

Why should this be in a world that has an abundance of resources and technology? I pondered this question while walking through the village of Neemramah on the edge of the Rajistan desert in India. The villagers had only rudimentary lighting and no running water. Though it was a weekday, I saw children in the streets. "Why aren't they in school?" I asked. The answer was that only the children of rich families went to school. This was not back in the 1960s or 1970s when my journeys had accustomed me to such sights; this was in 1998. A few days later, India tested a nuclear weapon.

How is it that India, soon to be the most populated country in the world, is ranked by the World Bank at 142 in terms of real per capita income, yet ranks first in the world in total arms imports? The most basic social services are often missing in both India and its neighbour Pakistan, which followed India in testing nuclear weapons. The rising defence burdens in these countries continue to impose prohibitive social and economic costs on their people. Defence expenditure exceeds spending on education and health in Pakistan by about a quarter. The majority of Pakistan's population is illiterate, and amongst females, illiteracy runs at 80 percent. In India, defence spending consumes two-thirds as many resources as does combined spending on education and health.

South Asia, fast emerging as the poorest, most illiterate, most malnourished area in the world, is now one of the most militarized regions. These trend lines have ominous implications for the world, considering that both India and Pakistan have become nuclear powers. The region contains nearly one-fifth of humanity. Just the increase in South Asia's population each year exceeds the total population of 50 smaller U.N. member countries.

The standing armies of South Asia employ more than two million soldiers, about 90 percent in India and Pakistan. In both countries, employment in the armed forces has become a major source of overall employment. The armed forces of India and Pakistan are a very disciplined group, possessing considerable skills. Why could not such skills be used in building the economic and social infrastructure both countries need so badly, such as rural-to-market roads, bridges, wells, lining of canals, basic health centres, schools, and other community facilities?

To ask these questions is to delve to the core of the human security dilemma. Government priorities for military spending are wildly disproportionate to expenditures on economic and social development at a time when the lack of development is now recognized as the most acute security threat facing the least developed States.

World Military Expenditures vs. OECD Official Development Assistance

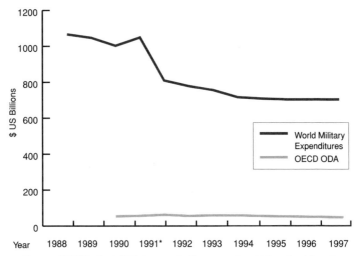

Source: *SIPRI Yearbook 1998: Armaments, Disarmament, and International Security* (Oxford: Oxford University Press, 1998); *The 1991 WME figure is from the U.S. Arms Control and Disarmament Agency as the figure was not available from SIPRI.

A Theft From the Poor

A double standard of immense proportions prevails, in which governments in one breath plead an inability to fund social needs because of deficits and in the next breath appropriate huge sums for warfare and its preparation. The very year following the Children's Summit, which amounted to applause-seeking rhetoric and little cash, governments suddenly found $60 billion to prosecute the Gulf War.

So powerful is the arms industry, and so all-pervading its influence, that it has seeped into nearly every aspect of society. Western countries spend $483 billion annually on defence but only $48 billion on Official Development Assistance, which is supposed to lift up the human security needs of the most destabilized areas of the world. Even this small amount of aid money is questioned, but the military appropriations go through the governmental processes unchallenged. The reality is that sustainable economic development could remove many pre-war tensions.

One man, a general and a president, did challenge this disparity but his words are not heard in government councils today. Dwight D. Eisenhower, in his final speech in 1961 as President of the United States, warned his countrymen against the unwarranted influence of "the military-industrial complex." Cast in stone above Eisenhower's tomb in Abilene, Kansas, are the words of a speech he delivered in 1953:

Every gun that is made, every warship launched, every rocket fired, signifies, in the final sense, a theft from those who hunger and are not fed, those who are cold and are not clothed. This world in arms is not spending money alone. It is spending the sweat of its laborers, the genius of its scientists, the hopes of its children.

So far has the U.S. moved from Eisenhower's words that it is actual U.S. policy to help domestic arms merchants get new contracts abroad. The influence of the Pentagon, in disbursing defence contracts throughout the country in order to spread jobs and build up local economies' dependence on military spending, is well established.

The modern world countenances trillions of dollars pumped into armaments while homelessness, starvation, and grinding poverty are the lot of hundreds of millions. In fact, after oil, the weapons industry is the world's number two industry. Roughly 70 percent of its investment comes from the North but the developing countries are spending unaffordable amounts on weapons at the expense of essential health care, medicines, vaccinations, clean water, sanitation, and other urgent social needs of large and vulnerable populations. All told, government military spending represents 12 percent of all government expenditures at a time when citizens of both developed and developing countries feel sharp cuts in social programs such as health, education, and day care.

The proposed U.N. plan of action to halt desertification in many tropical countries could be funded for a whole year by the $5 billion that represents two days of global military expenditure. The money spent in just 24 hours on the Gulf War could have funded a child immunization program for five years and prevented the deaths of five million children annually. For the cost of three Stealth bombers, the crippling debt of developing countries could be forgiven. Such spending demands the question, who is being secured? It is certainly not human beings. A visitor from another planet would stare in disbelief at the reasoning processes that produce such distortions.

A New Definition of Security

My thinking about these distortions has been influenced by Inga Thorsson, who, in 1982, led a United Nations study on the relationship of disarmament and development. An official in the Swedish foreign ministry, Inga Thorsson understood the meaning of Eisenhower's reference to "theft." Her report, which established a "dynamic triangular relationship" between disarmament, development, and security, led to a U.N. international conference on this theme. This conference, in turn, increased the world community's understanding that security today does not come out of the barrel of a gun but in building the economic and social conditions necessary to construct a functioning civil society within States, and a peaceful environment between them.

The dynamic triangular relationship is interrelated. The development process can enhance security and thereby promote arms reductions and disarmament. And disarmament, providing for security at progressively lower levels of armaments, could allow additional resources to be devoted to addressing nonmilitary challenges to security such as resource scarcity and economic marginalization, and thus result in enhanced overall human security. Disarmament and development become the twin bases for security based not simply on securing sovereign States, but human beings.

A number of U.N. international commissions of the 1980s, led by such figures as Willy Brandt, former Chancellor of Germany and Nobel Peace laureate, Olof Palme, former Prime Minister of Sweden, and Gro Harlem Brundtland, former Prime Minister of Norway and now head of the U.N. World Health Organization, reached similar conclusions. Countries are joined together by economic interdependence as well as by the threat of destruction. In the nuclear age, no nation can achieve true security by itself. Technology has made the traditional concept of national security obsolete. The world must find a way to cooperate in restructuring the international economic system. The commissions proposed many steps: broadening the decision-making processes of the international financial institutions (World Bank, International Monetary Fund (IMF)) so that the South would have more input, a system of international taxation to benefit the most vulnerable peoples, reduced spending on arms, and increased spending on health and education.

All these ideas were put out at the height of the Cold War, when popular wisdom held that high military spending and the nuclear weapons arms race were unassailable. When the Berlin Wall fell, a "peace dividend" was suddenly talked about. But, like the vision of a "new world order," the "peace dividend" fell by the wayside, unless you count the soaring stock market as the principal benefit for humanity in the post-Cold War era.

The "peace dividend" has not been realized by the United Nations, whose programs for peacekeeping, the alleviation of human suffering, and preventive diplomacy are so starved of the necessary governmental funding that they had to be rescued by the private beneficence of the media owner Ted Turner, who pledged $1 billion to U.N. work. Neither has the "peace dividend" been experienced by the poorest fifth of the world. So far are we from a genuine "peace dividend," in which the poor of the world would receive the benefits of enlarged spending on health and education, that the richest nations are actually subsidizing arms sales to poor countries. Health and

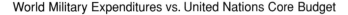

World Military Expenditures vs. United Nations Core Budget

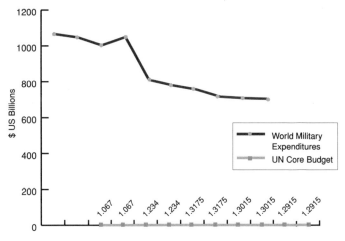

Year   1988 1989 1990 1991 1992 1993 1994 1995 1996 1997 1998 1999

Source: *SIPRI Yearbook 1998: Armaments, Disarmament, and International Security* (Oxford: Oxford University Press, 1998).

education can be cut in economic hard times, but arms sales must be protected. The political order continues to underwrite the culture of combat.

Continuing militarization results in an enormous drain on brainpower through investment in military research. Of the 2.25 million scientists involved in research worldwide, about 500,000 work on military research and development projects. Of physicists and engineers, more than 50 percent work exclusively on the development of weapons.

As far as providing jobs, military spending is a much worse investment than civilian projects. For example, U.N. analyses show that $1 billion spent on weapons, supplies, and services generates 25,000 jobs. The same $1 billion would create 30,000 mass transit jobs, 36,000 housing jobs, 41,000 education jobs, or 47,000 health care jobs.

With the end of the Cold War East-West arms race, major opportunities for conversion of military production to civilian programs exist. However, these opportunities are resisted by the military-industrial complex. The U.N. wants to do more to advance proposals for large-scale conversion, but is held back by major States where large sections of the population are dependent on military production. As the costs associated with the dismantling of American and Russian nuclear weapons have shown, disarmament creates short-term pain. In the short term, the costs of disarmament are dominant, but in the long term, benefits emerge. Disarmament would facilitate the release of scarce resources in the field of research and development. With resources freed from military research and development, new and old problems facing the global infrastructure for peace, such as continued social and economic injustices inflicted upon the poor and powerless, could be tackled.

Despite all the obstacles, Thorsson and the commissions that followed her have made an imprint on international thinking. When the one and only Summit (Heads of State) of the U.N. Security Council was held January 31, 1992, the world leaders issued a declaration containing a new analysis of what constitutes security:

The absence of war and military conflicts amongst States does not in itself ensure international peace and security. The non-military sources of instability in the economic, social, humanitarian and ecological fields have become threats to peace and security.

A new political understanding of the integrated agenda for global security was thus born. The U.N. has advanced, through a number of global conferences in the 1990s, public understanding of how arms reductions, economic and social development, environmental protection, and the advancement of human rights are all interlocked. In intellectual terms, this is an advance in the concept of security. It shows human progress.

But in political terms, the militarist mentality prevails. We have not been able to break free from the culture of war as the means of resolving interstate and intrastate conflict. A putative culture of peace struggles to find its way to the councils of the powerful.

Governments Dodge the Issue

In 1994, the U.N. convened a group of experts for "World Hearings on Development." The group stated that peace, security, and development are "inextricably linked." It had been hoped that, with the end of the Cold War, there would be not only a decrease in military expenditure in the developed countries but also a transfer of resources to the developing countries. "This hope has not been realized." The group insisted that security encompasses not just preventing an armed attack but also ensuring the safety, well-being, and basic rights of the world's citizens. Sustainable development is at the centre of this broader concept of security.

But as the five-year follow-up to the 1992 Earth Summit showed, there has been hardly any new money devoted to sustainable development. The shortfall in funding programs identified by the U.N. as vital to human security is not caused by a shortage of money, however much the deficit-ridden major governments like to advance this argument. The shortfall is caused by the wrong priorities in government spending, which continue to finance defence and military operations at exorbitantly high levels.

Governments of the North have dodged any post-Cold War discussion of the disarmament/development theme, even going so far as to keep it out of the Declaration and Program of Action of the 1995 World Summit for Social Development. This was the one U.N. document of the post-Cold War era that could have effectively highlighted new sources of funding to alleviate the distress of disadvantaged peoples. Instead it was left to a nongovernmental representatives to excoriate the "enormous waste" of human, natural, and financial resources caused by the continuation of militarization. "It causes further inequality and pauperization, political and social violence, including violations against women, and violent conflict that adds to the rising global death toll and the growing number of refugees and displaced people."

Almost two decades after the Thorsson study, the world finds itself in the same old sterile debate involving the relationship between disarmament and development. The U.S., which refused to attend the International Conference because it denied any relationship between disarmament and development, still prevents any meaningful U.N. action to follow up the conference. Meanwhile, the Official Development Assistance of the industrialized countries has actually dropped since 1992 in the face of the recurrence of conflict, and complex political and humanitarian emergencies, such as refugee flows and famine throughout Africa and several Asian countries. The Development Assistance Committee of the OECD, which monitors the flow of Western aid, piously insists, "We remain committed to generating substantial resources for development cooperation," all the while knowing that governments are falling further behind the international target of 0.7 percent of GNP. Were that target to be reached, an extra $100 billion would be available. The extra money represents 50 days' worth of current military spending.

A Path to "Sustainable Disarmament"

Jayantha Dhanapala, Under-Secretary-General of the U.N. for Disarmament, tries to approach the relationship in a new way, by talking about "sustainable disarmament." This idea begins by recognizing, as Thorsson did, that the world has a choice: it can continue to pursue destabilizing arms races or it can move towards a more stable and balanced social and economic development; it cannot do both. Next, the idea does away with the division of the world into nuclear haves and have-nots. The world must choose between a nuclear weaponized world and a nuclear-weapon-free world. The only sustainable choice is nuclear disarmament.

Then, in the field of conventional arms, the excesses justified under Article 51 of the U.N. Charter, which recognizes the right to self-defence, must be curbed by adherence to Article 26, which calls for the "least diversion for armaments of the world's human and economic resources."

The only hope for efforts for demobilization and de-weaponization of former combatants is to link them to community development projects that create employment and generate new income for poorer sections of society, particularly the youth. These approaches require more transparency of the international arms market, strong regulations to deter suppliers, and more intergovernmental cooperation in the sharing of information. Public demand to tighten controls on arms production is a necessary precondition to getting any meaningful government action.

It would help if governments would remember the analysis of the past 500 years by the historian Paul Kennedy, who attributed the fall of the greatest powers to excessive arms expenditures. Why cannot governments, working together, initiate more disarmament measures? That is what public opinion polls show people want. But the voracious demands of the military-industrial complex drive the arms production machinery. Advocates of sustainable disarmament must reach over their heads. Sustainable disarmament must appeal to the ideals and self-interests of a diverse spectrum of groups in society, especially the opinion-makers in government, industry, academia, the public interest community, and the news media. Finally, sustainable disarmament needs to be elaborated in government legislation, regulations, and policies that advance the disarmament objective.

Some progress in relating sustainable development to sustainable disarmament is being made. Led by Nobel Peace laureate Oscar Arias, former President of Costa Rica, a group of world leaders, both in governments and nongovernmental organizations, met in Brussels in 1998 to promote initiatives to stop the proliferation of small arms and light weapons as

World Spending Priorities 1996

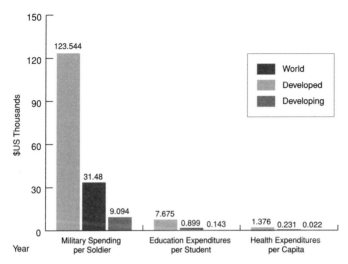

Source: Ruth Leger Sivard, *World Military and Social Expenditures 1996* (Washington, D.C.: World Priorities, 1996).

prerequisites to sustainable development. They called for national legislation to control the possession and transfer of small arms and light weapons; halt the abduction and involvement of children in armed forces; and promote post-conflict reconstruction and reconciliation in a stable and secure environment. A similar conference was held in Oslo to address the human suffering caused by the use of small arms in war–torn societies. It recommended tighter controls on manufacturing and transfer of weapons and more transparency through U.N. mechanisms.

Governments could do these things–if they had the will. Unfortunately, they are mired in what historian Barbara Tuchman called the "wooden-headedness" of governments. This wooden-headedness consists in assessing a situation in terms of preconceived fixed notions while ignoring or rejecting any contrary signs. It is acting according to wish while not allowing oneself to be deflected by the facts. As was said of Philip II of Spain: "No experience of the failure of his policy could shake his belief in its essential excellence." The modern leaders of NATO, which conducted a blundering bombing campaign against Serbia, should take note.

Government policy-makers must first get rid of their old ideas that security can be bought with enough weaponry. This idea belongs in the horse-and-buggy age. Only when they shift their thinking to the modern requirements of the integrated security agenda will they then be able to plan for a culture of peace. Such a new culture would challenge the glorification of weapons and foster the resolution of conflicts peacefully.

Later, I will expand on the benefits of a culture of peace. For now, I want to emphasize the need to recognize how continued excessive military spending, far from aiding security, actually jeopardizes human security in every area of the planet, rich and poor alike. Security today demands not more military spending to fight future wars but spending on health, education, family support, environment, and crime prevention to sow the seeds of peace. As a minimal first step, all governments should spend at least as much on health and education as on military programs.

Developed nations must contribute, actively and credibly, to the demilitarization of life, for no state that profits from war can convincingly argue for peace. It is not enough merely to admonish developing countries to cut their military expenditures. It is the developed countries of the North that bear the greatest responsibility: they are the biggest arms spenders and they have the greatest potential to promote world-wide human development.

The military-industrial complex continues to threaten our common future. It has been clearly established that poverty and social exclusion are one of the most important causes of modern armed conflicts. Yet the international community is doing little to build the conditions for peace. The "peace dividend" remains elusive.

Human Security
An Agenda for the
21st Century

Towards a Culture of Peace

4

When the United Nations observed its fiftieth anniversary in 1995, the General Assembly issued a Declaration pledging a strengthened U.N. for the 21st century. Four principal objectives were cited: peace, development, equality, and justice. Pleasant yet general comments were made about each of these elements of the global security agenda. Specifics were in short supply because, in order to produce a consensus document, the lowest common denominator of agreement had to be adhered to. The hard questions about what actually has to be done to achieve peace, development, equality, and justice were left for another day.

That day has arrived.

The window of opportunity for peace and human security opened by the fall of the Berlin Wall in 1989 is rapidly being closed. The reversion to militarism in the 1990s has been astonishing. The Gulf War, Somalia, Bosnia, the U.S. and U.K. bombing of Iraq, the NATO bombing of Kosovo and Serbia have all shown the continued reliance on militarism by government decision-makers. The development of instruments to build peace and security, thought to have been possible with the end of the Cold War, has been set back.

Nevertheless, the U.N. has provided a blueprint for peace. It now needs to be fleshed out. Enlightened self-interest must perceive that peace and security issues, economic and social justice issues, and environmental issues are interrelated.

Problems inter-lock and respect no borders. Organized crime, trafficking in children and drugs, the AIDS pandemic, desertification, ozone depletion all have to be dealt with. Problems that share the common denominator of poverty must be addressed: malnutrition, illiteracy, inadequate housing, and unemployment. Racism, ethnic strife, violence against women, political and social exclusion, and massive violations of human rights must be dealt with. And the incessant demand for more arms and recourse to military action in conflict resolution are continued barriers to peace.

A program of action at all levels—international, national, regional, and local—and real commitment to it is required. What follows are elements of a program of action.

Because an increasing number of nations will not tolerate the possession of nuclear weapons by some to the exclusion of others, the abolition of nuclear weapons is the indispensable condition for peace in the 21st century. While it is true that abolition must be part of broad and deep social change, there is no hope for an equitable world system as long as some powerful States retain nuclear weapons and try to prevent other States from acquiring them.

The adherents of nuclear weapons say that abolition will be the end result of the solidification of peace. They are wrong; the major States, through maintaining their nuclear weapons as instruments of power, actually are acting as a catalyst for the acquisition of nuclear weapons and thus destabilizing the regions of the world. Of course, a security architecture must be built to support the abolition of Nuclear Weapons, but it is the outright refusal of the Nuclear Weapon States to enter comprehensive negotiations for elimination that is worsening international relations.

Several proposals for a time-bound framework for the abolition of nuclear weapons have been made. In 1985, Mikhail Gorbachev, then the Soviet leader, proposed a 15-year plan, in three stages, that would have eliminated nuclear weapons by 2000. In 1988, India's Prime Minister, Rajiv Ghandi, later assassinated, proposed elimination by 2010. In 1996, a group of 28 nations tabled in the Conference on Disarmament in Geneva a three-phase Program of Action for elimination by 2020. Then came the New Agenda Coalition seeking an "unequivocal commitment" to elimination by the nuclear powers. The consistent reaction of the Western nuclear powers has been to dismiss such proposals. The farthest they have gone is to pledge "systematic and progressive efforts to reduce nuclear weapons globally, with the ultimate goal of eliminating those weapons." But, as the preparatory meetings for the 2000 Review of the Non-Proliferation Treaty have shown, even this weak pledge is not being adhered to. That is why the Middle Powers Initiative is stepping up its actions in exerting pressures on the NWS.

Advancing Abolition of Nuclear Weapons

The movement to abolish nuclear weapons is growing. The 1995 indefinite extension of the NPT is a cornerstone in building a new and long sought-after security architecture for the world. The extension underscored that all 187 NPT signatories have a role to play in ridding the world of nuclear weapons. A new fusion of strength by like-minded governments and the advanced wave of civil society can create enormous world pressure that the NWS will not be able to ignore.

Movement forward is essential to preserve the integrity of the NPT. Just the expressed willingness of the NWS to engage in negotiations would uplift the world mood. It would keep open the window of opportunity to build a better system for world security than relying on nuclear deterrence. "Systematic" progress on nuclear elimination that can be measured will keep the world community from splitting apart on this pivotal issue. No other issue is as divisive or complex; that is why many want to avoid it. But it must be faced now, for meaningful progress on other disarmament issues is not possible while a nuclear stalemate persists.

Nuclear weapons fly in the face of a just world order. They are representative of an intellectual and diplomatic paralysis. Nuclear weapons, by holding the world hostage as they do, are the pinnacle of organized violence. The campaign for abolition cannot operate alone. It must be part of organized movements to prevent war; fortunately, there are many such movements, embracing diplomatic initiatives and civil society initiatives. New techniques of early warning of incipient conflict, preventive diplomacy, peacemaking, and peace-building are available. Regional organizations, such as the Organization for Security and Cooperation in Europe, are in place to strengthen the U.N. system. The fullness of this system is providing the basis for an expanding body of international law that could, in time, support a Nuclear Weapons Convention prohibiting the production and deployment of nuclear weapons. The system must be nourished, so that it matures into a credible and reliable force for peace.

Powerful new tools to prevent war include confidence-building measures, transparency and information exchange, mutual constraints on force deployments, negotiated reductions in armed forces, and restrictions on the arms trade. These steps, combined with increased use of mediation and judicial processes, are all worthy, but they are fragmented. A new civil society organization, Global Action to Prevent War, believes it is time to bring together diverse approaches into a unified program to prevent war. Such a program would include conventional force reductions, limits on arms production and trade, cuts in military spending, measures to stop proliferation and build confidence, training for peaceful conflict resolution, and means for peace-building and peacekeeping.

A comprehensive approach is needed both to be effective in reducing armed conflict and to mobilize sustained public pressure for new policies. Such an approach, reflecting new ways of thinking, new understandings and new solutions to security, will strengthen existing peacemaking and disarmament programs by building a broader coalition of interested public and government officials to support them. Once convinced that a practical program to prevent war that recognizes complementary ideas of security exists, people and governments will be more likely to champion this more enlightened and humane view.

By lowering the level of armed conflict, such a comprehensive program will fulfil an essential requirement for eliminating all nuclear weapons. In fact, neither program can be fully implemented without the active contribution of the other. Achievement of nuclear disarmament will require reduced levels of conflict worldwide and effective ways of reducing the conventional forces of the major powers. Countries like Russia, China, and India will not relinquish their nuclear weapons if the main effect of doing so is to enhance the already large conventional superiority of the United States. Correspondingly, governments will not be ready to drastically cut national armed forces unless nuclear weapons are on their way to elimination.

The major States customarily object to timelines to implement disarmament treaties. What is wrong with timelines to achieve such a noble goal for the world? Timelines are used in every business enterprise. They make sense. They enable progress to be checked. They provide confidence that steps to a larger end product are actually being achieved and give heart to continue past remaining obstacles.

It might take 50 years to build a permanent global security system. But taken in bite sizes, people would take heart that movement to fulfil a vision is occurring. Global Action to Prevent War sees a ten-year Phase One by giving to a strengthened U.N. and regional security organizations improved capabilities for conflict resolution, peacekeeping and defence against aggression and genocide. Protection of human rights and enforcement of the rule of law as stipulated by the U.N. Security Council would be stepped up.

A second 10-year phase would bring substantial cuts in armed forces and military spending, and in arms production and trade. There would be mandatory submission of disputes to the International Court of Justice. A tax on international financial transactions would support these activities.

A third phase of similar length would entail a commitment by nations (including the major powers) not to deploy their armed forces beyond national borders except in multilateral actions under the mandate of the Security Council. This commitment would test global and regional institutions while participants still have national means of action as a fallback.

The fourth and final phase would complete the process of making war rare and brief by permanently transferring to the U.N. and regional organizations the authority and capability for armed intervention to prevent or end war and genocide. Individually recruited, all-volunteer armed forces would be maintained by the U.N. Deep cuts would be made in national forces, which would be cut back to air defence, coast guard, and border guards. U.N. forces, and those maintained by regional security organizations would have the police functions of guarding against re-armament and transnational violence by terrorists or criminal syndicates.

Though long-term, and too easily dismissed by those who cannot see past the shackles of militarism that perpetuate war, this program is practical in seriously addressing the chaos that characterizes the world's quest for peace today. A chief value lies in cutting across regional economic disparities with steps that enhance common security. Throughout the various phases would be interwoven steps to reduce nuclear weapons and, even more important, reduce the dependence on nuclear weapons as the means of security. The actual year in which the last nuclear weapon is dismantled or the precise time when the international community recognizes that war is no longer a viable means of resolving disputes is less important than the decision taken today to start down that road. The refusal of States to recognize that war is outmoded and a new architecture of global security must be built leaves the world in an increasingly dangerous condition.

War Is Not Inevitable

Sequenced steps, making war rare along the way, will save thousands of lives and huge sums of money. By releasing funds, energy, and attention from military matters, the program would strengthen ongoing efforts to rectify injustice, meet basic human needs, and build tolerance. More broadly, it would foster the democratic institutions that must replace armed force in resolving conflicts. For security can no longer be simply conceived as a zero-sum competition that detracts from the cooperative steps required in fostering a culture of peace. The length of time required to achieve this goal should not deter us from starting now. It would fill the world with hope to see a program aimed at reducing the frequency of organized armed conflict. Without such a program, the killing will continue.

It is often said that war is inevitable, it is part of our human nature, people have been fighting throughout history. This is a superficial analysis. Human beings are not genetically programmed for war. There is no inherent biological component of our nature that produces violence. When I hold my tiny grandchildren in my arms and look into their faces, I do not see some lurking evil, waiting only to mature in order to strike out. Rather, I see a person wanting to be loved, fed, cared for and who responds favourably to love and affection. If my grandchildren become violent when they mature it will be because they were socialized to violence, that they accepted violence out of desperation, or because they saw others doing so. UNESCO points out that war begins in our minds; so too must the new idea, so necessary in the technological age of mass destruction, that peace begins in our minds.

The present pessimism must be lifted by the recognition that war is not inevitable. Violence on the scale of what we have seen in Bosnia, Rwanda, Somalia, Kosovo, and elsewhere does not emerge inexorably from human interaction. Because the hatred and incitement to violence fostered by social and economic inequality, combined with the readily available supply of deadly weapons, are so evident, it is essential and urgent to find ways to prevent disputes from turning massively violent. The real problem here is not that we do not know about incipient and large-scale violence, it is that often we do not know how to act. Either we ignore mass killings if the area concerned is not central to our interests, or, as in the case of Kosovo, we unleash a rain of destruction in the name of saving humanity.

Examples from "hot spots" around the world illustrate that the potential for violence can be diffused through the early, skillful, and integrated application of political, diplomatic, economic, and military measures. Though terrible suffering occurred, it is a fact that warring parties have put down their arms in El Salvador, Namibia, Mozambique, South Africa, Guatemala, and the Philippines. The peace accords in Northern Ireland and the Middle East, though precarious, illustrate that the human desire for peace can overcome the histories of conflict. Since 1945, the U.N. has actually negotiated 172 peaceful settlements that have ended regional conflicts, including an end to the Iran-Iraq war and the withdrawal of Soviet troops from Afghanistan.

These lessons have taught us that violence and war are not inevitable. An unavoidable clash of civilizations is not our fate. War and mass violence usually result from deliberate political decisions. Rather than intervening in violent conflicts after they have erupted and then engaging in post-conflict peace-building, it is more humane and more efficient to prevent such violence in the first place by addressing its economic, social, cultural, and ethnic roots. This is the essence of a culture of peace approach.

The continuing work of UNESCO in promoting knowledge of a culture of peace is inspiring. Responding to a request by the U.N. General Assembly to develop the concept of a culture of peace as an integral approach to preventing violence and armed conflicts,

UNESCO succeeded in defining norms, values, and aims of peace. A culture of peace is the set of values, attitudes, traditions, modes of behaviour, and ways of life that reflect and inspire:

• Respect for life and for all human rights.

• Rejection of violence in all its forms and commitment to the prevention of violent conflicts by tackling their root causes through dialogue and negotiation.

• Commitment to full participation in the process of equitably meeting the developmental and environmental needs of present and future generations.

• Promotion of the equal rights and opportunities of women and men.

• Recognition of the rights of everyone to freedom of expression, opinion, and information.

• Devotion to the principles of freedom, justice, democracy, tolerance, solidarity, cooperation, pluralism, cultural diversity, dialogue, and understanding between nations, between ethnic, religious, cultural, and other groups, and between individuals.

It can readily be seen that a culture of peace is a process of individual, collective, and institutional transformation. It grows out of beliefs and actions of the people themselves and develops in each country within its specific historical, socio-cultural, and economic context. A key is the transformation of violent competition into cooperation based on the sharing of values and goals. In particular, it requires that conflicting parties work together to achieve objectives of common interests at all levels, including the development process.

A peace consciousness does not appear overnight. It is evident that constructing a culture of peace requires comprehensive educational, social, and civic action. It addresses people of all ages. An open-minded, global strategy is required to make a culture of peace take root in people's hearts and minds.

The General Assembly has helped to foster this ethical transformation by proclaiming the year 2000 as the International Year for the Culture of Peace. Mobilizing public opinion and developing new education programs at all levels are essential to promoting society's rejection of war.

The Hague Appeal for Peace

These ideas were powerfully expressed at the 1999 Hague Appeal for Peace where 7,000 people of 100 nationalities gathered for a four-day "jamboree" of seminars, exhibits, concerts, and a general outpouring of human yearning for peace. They cheered when U.N. Secretary-General Kofi Annan said: "The ultimate crime is not to give away some real or imaginary national interest. The ultimate crime is to miss the chance for peace, and so condemn your people to the unutterable misery of war."

The Hague Appeal was held on the hundredth anniversary of the first such meeting. In 1899, 108 delegates from 26 countries gathered in response to an invitation by Nicholas II, Czar of Russia, to discuss ways of halting the arms race. The conference was driven by Russia's desire to escape the crushing burden of keeping up with the pace of armament in Western Europe, particularly Germany and England. The conference produced the "Hague Convention," which remains to this day one of the most important sources of international law. A second Hague Peace Conference was held in 1907. It laid the basis for a third great meeting to be backed by civil society around the world. But the guns of August 1914 interfered with the holding of the conference. Wars and turmoil for the rest of the century prevented the holding of the third conference until 1999.

The new Hague Appeal challenges the assumption of today's skeptics who have given up on the essential U.N. idea that succeeding generations can be saved from the scourge of war. The Hague Appeal launched a citizens' "Agenda for Peace and Justice in the 21st Century," in which citizen advocates, progressive governments, and official agencies work together for common goals.

To build a culture of peace, The Hague Appeal has highlighted these themes:

- *Traditional Failure:* Move beyond the traditional approaches to preventing war, which have failed disastrously. Big-power bullying tactics are not diplomacy. Sanctions that starve the poor are not solidarity. Fire-brigade peacekeeping efforts are no substitute for early warning systems.

- *Human Security:* Security must be redefined in terms of human and ecological needs instead of national sovereignty and national borders. This requires new priorities for sustainable development instead of armaments.

- *All Human Rights for All Peace:* The violation of human rights is one of the root causes of war. These violations include the denial of economic, social, and cultural rights as well as political and civil rights. The artificial distinction between these two sets of rights can no longer be tolerated.

- *Soft Power:* Civil society and progressive governments are choosing "soft power" paths, utilizing negotiation, coalition building and new diplomacy methods of settling disputes, while rejecting the "hard power" dictates of major powers, including militaries and economic conglomerates.

- *Rule of Law:* Universal adherence to international law must be developed by the collaboration of States that recognize that modern problems cannot be solved by merely domestic laws. Current instruments, such as the International Court of Justice and the new International Criminal Court, must be invigorated.

- *Initiatives in Peace-Making:* Too often, peace initiatives are proposed only as a last resort and negotiations restricted to disputants. Civil society should also convene peace initiatives before a crisis gets out of control and lives are lost.

- *Democratic Decision-Making:* In recent years, the U.N. system, created to be a universal force for peace, has been treated with cynicism, politicized and under-funded. The international system must be revived, made more multilateral, and provided with resources if it is to realize its potential in peace-building. The U.N. Security Council must serve human security rather than Great Power interests.

- *Humanitarian Intervention:* Speedy and effective intervention of military forces, mandated by the Security Council, are required where civilians are threatened by genocide, war crimes, crimes against humanity, and extreme national disasters. A standing U.N. intervention force must be established.

- *Money for Peace:* Billions are spent on arms and militarization, while worthwhile peace initiatives and programs for human security are starved from lack of funds. These priorities must be reversed.

Strengthened by these powerful themes, The Hague Appeal for Peace launched specific campaigns to reduce the trade in small arms, obtain universal ratification of the Landmines Treaty, boost the International Criminal Court, seek an unequivocal commitment from the Nuclear Weapons States to begin comprehensive negotiations for the elimination of nuclear weapons, start a phased campaign to reduce military establishments over a period of years, promote a worldwide coalition of peace forces for humanitarian intervention, stop the recruitment and use of children under eighteen in hostilities, and campaign to make universal peace education compulsory in primary and secondary schools and in teacher education.*

Without a doubt, powerful forces opposing these campaigns still drive government policy-making. The old ways of preparing for peace through war die hard. We should not expect an easy conversion of the "realists" who do not yet see that peace is obtained through preparing for peace. Nonetheless, The Hague Appeal for Peace successfully redefined peace as not only the absence of conflict between and within States, but also the absence of economic and social injustice. Understanding the integrated agenda for peace, the Hague enterprise fused environmental activists, human rights advocates, feminists, spiritual leaders, humanitarian aid and development workers, and experts in disarmament to work together for the development of a sustainable culture of peace.

What we are now witnessing is a "new diplomacy" that addresses the diffusion of security threats with regional institutions and smaller units of civil society such as nongovernmental organizations. The sources of problem-solving and decision-making are increasingly shared by national governments, supra-national and subnational institutions, all tiered at the global, regional, and community levels. The dynamism and effectiveness of such an approach has been seen in such initiatives as the Earth Summit in Rio, the Social Development Summit in Copenhagen, and the Women's Conference in Beijing as well as the Ottawa Process to Ban Landmines. With such agendas and a good dose of imagination, stamina, and moral courage, civil society working with friendly governments on practical plans, such as the process that developed the Landmines Treaty, could create a 21st century culture of peace.

* All these campaigns are looking for people to join them. More information can be obtained from The Hague Appeal for Peace Website: http://www.haguepeace.org/. Specific requests for information can be obtained by e-mail: New York hap99@igc.org or IBP Zurich mailbox@ipb.org.

The Right to Human Development

5

The contrast between government rhetoric and performance in ending the worst forms of poverty is stunning. Yet an agenda for development that can be sustained through the 21st century is slowly taking shape. Political will needs to be energized to make this agenda a reality, because development is a crucial component of international security.

The statistics of poverty in the world, real as they are, seem to discourage people, or make them cynical, that anything can be done about this. It is important, therefore, to recognize that a great deal has been done.

Since 1960, child death rates in developing countries have been cut by more than half. Per capita food production and consumption have risen by 20 percent. Malnutrition rates have declined by almost one-third. The percentage of people with access to clean water has doubled to 70 percent. Adult literacy has risen from less than half to about two-thirds.

But in this four-decade period, world population has doubled and 80 percent of this growth has been in the developing countries. The gap between the rich and poor in this time period has trebled so that the poorest, who are greater in numbers than ever before, are poorer by relative standards. The poorest today have few championing their cause, since it is now widely believed in the new age of globalization and technological innovation that the poor have only themselves to blame for their distress. "They have not kept up."

Of course, the poor have not kept up with the strong, who are racing to ever new heights. The staggering growth in wealth disparities, both between and within countries, the approach of ecological limits, and the unmet expectations of an increasingly young and urban global population are a prelude to social dynamite. According to the 1996 U.N. Human Development Report, "If present trends continue, economic disparities between industrialized and developing countries will move from the inequitable to the inhuman."

The poor have been marginalized in the decision-making processes, they have suffered cutbacks in social programs, and they are the victims of their countries' staggering debt burdens. Despite these setbacks, the poor have gained a principle. It may be true that they cannot eat the principle today, but it does give them a source of hope for tomorrow—because that principle is their rights.

Since the early 1990s, human rights have played a prominent role in international development cooperation. United Nations' documents now affirm that development is a fundamental human right. The 1993 U.N. World Conference on Human Rights states: "The right to development is an inalienable human right and an integral part of fundamental human freedoms." This means, in practice, that people have a right to food, water, and health and education facilities in order to maintain and develop their own lives. The reason this gain, even if yet confined to a declaration, is so important is because it moves the subject of international development from charity to justice.

Human development is no longer something that ought to be done. It must be done. Just as it is now taken for granted that the civil and political rights of a person must be protected by law, so too the protection of the poor against starvation, malnourishment, disease, and ignorance will find its way into the legislative and judicial arenas.

With this advance in thinking has come another: development is the most secure basis for peace. The U.N. Security

Council's definition of global security specifically includes economic and social development as a prerequisite. Several U.N. conferences dealing with global problems have highlighted the crucial links between the three goals of the U.N. Charter: peace, development, and human rights.

As the rise in low-intensity conflicts the world over shows, the most prevalent threats to international security have to do with social and economic injustices inflicted upon the poor and the powerless. Expanding the definition of security beyond the military context to include a commitment to protecting the biosphere on economic and environmental grounds and the equitable distribution of the planet's resources equips us to meet future challenges to world stability. Development therefore must now be understood as integral to building the conditions for peace.

This new understanding of the economic and social extension of universal human rights as a basis for peace is an advance of historic importance. Arguments for the right to an adequate standard of living, the right to education, the right to work and to equal pay for equal work now can be made on the double claim of justice and the political strengthening of civil society. This approach puts people at the centre of the development process. While this may seem obvious to some, it is actually a breakthrough. For a long time, the development process was centered on physical infrastructure as the key to development. Put in enough airports, harbours, bridges, and roads and society would be uplifted. This top-down approach did not cure poverty because it left the poor where they were: hungry, jobless, ill, and living in misery. This approach lay behind a Brazilian president's quip that "Brazil is doing fine, but the people are doing badly."

Only when governments started directing development resources to health, education, and marketing improvements for the poor did real human development start to occur. On my first visit in 1977 to Bangladesh, one of the poorest countries in the world, I went through village after village of misery; yet the government pointed to airports and harbours as signs of development. In latter years, on my visits back to Bangladesh, I was struck by the improvements in village life and the sight of so many well-dressed, educated women playing an economic role in society never known before.

This shift in emphasis from self-serving state-based development to people has been building for some time and was highlighted at the World Summit for Social Development. Promoting a people-centered framework for social development and justice, the governments committed themselves to the goal of eradicating poverty as an ethical, social, political, and economic imperative of humankind. They agreed to take immediate steps to ensure that people living in poverty have access to productive resources, including credit, land, education, technology, information, and public services. They also agreed to ensure that national budgets and policies are oriented to meeting the basic needs of all people, reducing inequalities and targeting poverty as a strategic objective.

This was an undoubted achievement, but the specifics in how to raise new money to address the global poverty issue were lacking. Moving away from generalities would have destroyed the consensus.

Getting Debt Off Their Backs

An agenda for development must also address debt relief for the poorest countries. External debt is a millstone around the neck of many developing countries, which owe $1.3 trillion to northern institutions. The dramatic increase in multilateral debt began when the International Monetary Fund and the World Bank bailed out the commercial creditors no longer willing to lend to developing countries; debtor countries were forced to take World Bank and IMF-imposed lending packages to pay off commercial bank debt or risk default. In order to pay off the international financial institutions, developing countries cut back on health, education, and other services needed by the poor.

The human cost of the debt burden has been crushing. The governments of sub-Saharan Africa transfer to northern creditors four times as much as they spend on the health of their citizens. In Uganda, where one in five children do not reach their fifth birthday because of rampant disease, $3 per person is spent on health compared to $17 on debt repayments. The situation is the same in much of Latin America, where health and emergency response systems were utterly incapable of coping with the impact of Hurricane Mitch in 1998 due to debt repayments. The international community tolerates these inequities so that the narrow financial interests of creditors can be protected, subjecting indebted countries to the intervention of the IMF and World Bank in the management of priorities and the ruthless slashing of social expenditures. Those who lose their access to education, health services, and the social safety net suffer further marginalization and disempowerment.

The injustice of this situation has led to churches appealing for debt forgiveness as the only way out for the poorest developing countries. The G8 (the group of major economic powers) addressed this problem at their 1999 Summit and instituted forgiveness programs for the most heavily indebted totaling $27 billion. But this was only one-fifth the cancellation sought by such advocates as the Canadian Ecumenical Jubilee Initiative. A few countries, such as Canada, have partially forgiven loans. But the debt crisis deepens as entire countries reduce their capacity to make their citizens literate or reduce infant mortality in order to meet the standards of the structural adjustment programs imposed by the powerful. Indebted countries are condemned to endemic poverty and low productivity. This immorality must be recognized and remedied by the international community.

The debt crisis resulted from a model of development that did not put people first, a model that, in fact, increased the disparities between rich and poor. While steps to improve debt rescheduling programs and the cancellation of debt are critical, the real resolution of the problem demands reform of the international financial system, which precipitated the crisis in the first place.

Fundamental reform was tried in the 1970s, but did not work. The U.N. General Assembly adopted a document called the New International Economic Order (NIEO). This called for global negotiations between the North and South on key economic issues, such as access to resources, development assistance, and greater participation by the South in the decision-making processes of the international financial institutions. The structural reforms called for by the NIEO would have greatly benefited the poorest countries. But the negotiations never took place; the South wanted them to be held in the General Assembly where their full voice could be heard, and the North wanted them in the international financial institutions where they had the control.

Thus, in ensuing years, the South had to depend mainly on private investment by the North in sectors where immediate return could be produced. This skewed many of their economies. It enabled the stronger countries to "lift off." But the poorer countries were left behind. The new "tigers" led the way for a while, but later suffered severe setbacks when monetary systems collapsed. The poorer countries never received much investment in the first place and have always needed Official Development Assistance.

There is a strong moral imperative in providing aid in order to alleviate the extreme poverty and human suffering that still afflicts more than one billion people. Also, since all people are made less secure by the poverty and misery that exists in the world, the development of poor societies contributes to world security. And donor countries have a self-interest in fostering increased prosperity in developing countries so that they can become viable members of the international community and potentially stronger trading partners.

The Tobin Tax

Though aid is needed and ought to be maintained, it is an illusion to think that ODA, which currently amounts to only $48 billion a year, lifts the poorest out of their misery. New sources of money for economic and social development of vast populations in developing countries must be found. The very words "international" taxation raise the hackles of the rich and powerful who have, so far, been able to keep the idea on the library shelves. But the need for taxation to finance a proper development agenda for the 21st century is growing.

One man, James Tobin, an American Nobel laureate in economics, has given his name to a proposal that has received much attention. In 1978, Tobin first proposed the idea of a tax on foreign exchange transactions that would be applied uniformly by all major countries. About $1.5 trillion worth of currency is traded every day in unregulated financial markets. Because the volume is so high, even an infinitesimal tax, e.g., 0.1 percent, could yield over $175 billion. This would provide an enormous new pool of money for development projects around the world.

The tax would be low enough not to have a significant effect on longer term investment where yield is higher, but it would cut into yields of speculators moving mass amounts of currency around the world as they seek profit from minute differentials in currency fluctuations. This kind of financial speculation plays havoc with national budgets, economic planning, and the allocation of resources. A small tax would reduce the volatility of exchange rate fluctuations and provide exporters, importers, and long-term investors a more stable exchange rate in return for paying the tax.

The Tobin tax, on its own merits, would contribute to stabilizing the world economy. But considering what it could provide to enhance human security, it is an idea that should be warmly embraced. The governments of Australia and France have welcomed the proposal, the 18 member countries of the

Asia-Pacific Economic Cooperation forum have studied it, and a private Member's Motion in the Canadian House of Commons endorsed it. But the United States government is adamantly opposed and forced the United Nations Development Programme, an advocate, to stop producing new literature on the subject.

Objectors to the Tobin tax say it is unworkable, a political consensus could never be found, and there would be no agreement on who would administer it. The real reason for the objection is that this is seen as an infringement on a free market. Thus powerful bankers and investment companies, with massive political clout, have stiffened their resistance.

This is the same kind of resistance that weakened the U.N. Convention on the Law of the Sea, an international document signed in 1982 that contained a provision that the wealth contained in rich mineral deposits at the bottom of oceans would belong to the common heritage of humanity. The richest nations refused to ratify the Law of the Sea until this provision was excised to allow the countries with the technological capacity to extract the mineral wealth for themselves.

The finding of new sources of money to be used for the good of humanity does not have many supporters among the rich. Javier Perez de Cuellar, former Secretary-General of the United Nations, once proposed that, since the arms trade was not being curbed, arms transactions should be taxed with the benefits going to the poor. Arms merchants did not even bother mounting a campaign against this rather idealistic suggestion.

Other ideas for international taxation have been advanced by the Commission on Global Governance, a group of eminent world figures who, in 1995, recommended ways to improve the governance of the world. Far from recommending one world government (which if it ever came about would have the power of taxation), the Commission urged national governments to work in more innovative, cooperative ways to build common security. The Commission set out principles to broaden the base for financing global projects. First, it is appropriate to charge for the use of some common global resources, using market instruments. Second, the whole burden should not fall on a small number of industrial countries but should be spread. Third, new revenue systems should not substitute for domestic taxes but represent additional sources. In addition to the Tobin tax, the Commission suggested:

- A surcharge on airline tickets for use of increasingly congested flight lanes.

- A charge on ocean maritime transport, reflecting the need for ocean pollution control.

- User fees for noncoastal fishing, reflecting the pressures on many stocks and the costs of research and surveillance.

- Parking fees for geostationery satellites.

The ideas for global taxation not only address today's problems, they bring into sharper focus the need for sustainable development. Like taxation itself, sustainable development is highly controversial. Its usual meaning is a development process that meets the needs and aspirations of the present without compromising the ability to meet those of the future. When the pressures of population growth, consumption, and pollution are viewed in their inter-relationship, it is hard to see how the patterns of development that characterize Western society can be sustained—either in the sense of extending that kind of development around the world today, or into the future.

If the Western model were to become the global model, and if world population were to reach 10 billion during the next century, as the United Nations projects, the effect would be devastating. If, for example, the world had one car for every two people in 2050, as in North America today, there would be close to five billion cars. Given the congestion, pollution, and the fuel, material, and land requirements of the current global fleet of some 500 million cars, a global fleet of five billion would be catastrophic. Similarly, a world of ten billion consuming a diet on North American standards would require a harvest four times greater than the Earth's current levels. When pollution levels are then factored into an expanding economic model that is based on the past, the limits of the biosphere's capacity to sustain economic growth will be challenged severely, if not exceeded as is already happening in some cases.

Sustainable Development For All

Sustainable development is not possible without a redefinition of the word "development." Is the full use of the planet's resources by the strong development? Does development occur when vast numbers cannot access the processes of human betterment?

Development, properly understood, cannot be separated from human rights. Development is a value-loaded process. The recognition of this in the declarations and literature of the manifold U.N. global conferences is an important milestone. The fact that the world community, or at least the business element thereof that drives the legislative processes, is still resisting the idea of new forms of international taxation to stimulate equitable growth does not invalidate the idea. The affluent have always resisted the inauguration of tax-based domestic social security nets; yet those nets were put in place by national governments that bowed to the twin pressures of economic stability and public demand. Now economic and social problems sweep across borders and there is already a technological, if not a human, unity. Good governance requires the application of resources, financial and otherwise, for the common good in the name of common security.

A basic fact has emerged from the dislocations of the world economy and marginalization of the poor: governance cannot be sound unless it sustains human development. The goal of governance activities should be to develop capacities that are needed to realize development that gives priority to the poor, advances women, sustains the environment, and creates needed opportunities for employment and other livelihoods.

Human development should be seen, then, as expanding the choices for all people in society—particularly the poor and vulnerable—while protecting the natural systems on which all life depends. The human being stands at the centre of the development process. The new recognition of this essential truth provides hope that, gradually, the political, business, and legislative powers will recognize that development must be financed with adequate resources. The resources are not in short supply, the political will is.

The time is overdue to create a global forum that can provide leadership in economic, social, and environmental fields, a body that would have the same standing in relation to international economic matters that the Security Council has in peace and security matters. Thus, the Commission on Global Governance proposed an Economic Security Council (ESC), which would be elected by U.N. member states; there would be no veto power in such a body. At first, its principal function would be to continually assess the overall state of the world economy and provide a long-term strategic policy framework to promote stable, balanced, and sustainable development. The ESC would give political leadership on economic threats to security, such as shared ecological crises, economic instability, rising unemployment, mass poverty, and food shortages. As a deliberative body meeting at the highest political levels, the ESC could well evolve into that global negotiating forum on North-South issues that has proved so elusive.

The agenda for development in the 21st century needs a central driving force. This force can find its expression in the recognition that development and security are inter-related. It will therefore be increasingly necessary to cross sectoral, national, and institutional boundaries in order to construct partnerships for viable sustainability. In this vein, the broader conception of security and development is as necessary as it is opportune. The political demand for it will grow only when other U.N. goals such as equality and justice are better understood.

Pushing Equitable Global Standards

6

Not a day goes by without televised scenes of warfare, famine, murder, expulsions of people, and ethnic cleansing. Attacks on fundamental freedoms are common. Racism and intolerance ravage populations.

Bombarded by these images of immense cruelties, it is sometimes difficult to recognize that the world is also witnessing the birth of a culture of human rights. Though violent conflicts persist, billions still live in dehumanizing poverty and millions are forced to flee from their homes, there is a new political recognition that respect for human rights is essential to the sustainable achievement of peace, development, and democracy.

In the past half-century, since the adoption of the Universal Declaration of Human Rights, a vast range of vulnerable groups have been brought under the protection of human rights laws and new standards. Centuries-old patterns of discrimination and oppression have been broken. The extension of democracy to a great proportion of the world's peoples is a product of the extension of human rights. Apartheid is a thing of the past, and the decolonization process is nearly complete. A permanent International Criminal Court to prosecute those who perpetuate genocide, war crimes, and crimes against humanity has come into existence.

The subjects of rights have been clearly defined: rights of stateless persons, refugees, women, children, disabled persons,

persons with mental illness, prisoners, migrant workers, and indigenous peoples. The areas of protection have become increasingly precise: punishment of genocide, abolition of slavery, efforts to combat torture and to eliminate all forms of discrimination based on race, sex, religion, or belief. These aspirations, launched in the minds of men and women throughout the world—even if yet not fully reached—are perhaps the most powerful and inspirational force in modern history.

The development of the universality of human rights has reached a point where it is less urgent to define new rights than to persuade governments to adopt existing instruments and apply them effectively. There is now general acceptance of the importance of eliminating economic deprivation and recognition of social responsibility in this area. However grievous the violations still are, the newly understood idea of equality, as spelled out in the human rights declaration and covenants, is a keystone of the 21st century agenda for peace and security.

When the U.N.'s Fiftieth Anniversary Declaration came to this subject, the drafters put it under the heading, "Equality." The Declaration affirmed the dignity and worth of the human person and the equal rights of men and women, reaffirming that all human rights are universal, indivisible, interdependent, and interrelated; it is the duty of States to protect these rights. Governments went on to say they would protect these rights and freedoms; ensure the full and equal participation of women in all spheres of political, civil, economic, social, and cultural life; protect the rights of the child, persons with disabilities, the aged, indigenous peoples, refugees, and persons of national, ethnic and other minorities.

The concept of universal human rights in the broad general sense of entitlements of every human being is a relatively new idea. Before the Universal Declaration was adopted in 1948, the concept of entitlement was not understood. And when it was advanced, some said it was only a Western concept. While some parts of rights are found in ancient Western traditions, they are not exclusively Western in their antecedence. Non-Western ancient traditions also contained elements of rights. The modern assertion of individual human rights does clash with the rigidity of a State's rights over all else. The modern movement assigns to individuals a higher claim to the protection of their rights than to preserving the prerequisites of a nation state.

If the right to protection against genocide is universal, then that right is greater than the right of a state to determine which race will live within its borders. Thus the preservation of human rights challenges national sovereignty. The new phenomenon of the international community trying to decide when to intervene in internal massacres is a step forward for humanity because, in the past, foreigners seldom cared about the internal disputes within countries.

The idea that a "clash of civilizations" is inevitable because of fundamentally different interpretations of rights should be discarded. It leads to an intellectual and political closure that ignores the fact that people everywhere want the same things: food, water, healthy conditions, and an opportunity to develop their own lives. Modern conflict comes less from cultural mores and more from deprivation of these inherent desires and basic human needs. In short, the recognition of universal human rights gives the world common ground to stand on. It creates a basis of cooperation over the individual self-interest of States.

A significant obstacle to translating this new concept into political programs is that human rights are often presented, as the U.N. Declaration did, in terms of equality. While this word has rhetorical values, it is not precise. We are not all equal in the world. Some people are born with high intelligence and some are born with low intelligence. Some are born with handicaps, some without. A distinction should be made between equality and sameness. I interpret the word equality to mean equitability. A concern for equity, therefore, is not tantamount to an insistence on equality, but it does call for deliberate efforts to reduce gross inequalities and to promote a fairer sharing of resources.

The most dramatic example of lack of equitability is the growing gap between the rich and poor. The North, containing a fifth of the world population, controls 80 percent of the wealth and resources; the south, with four-fifths of world population, has only 20 percent of the wealth and resources. This is not only unjust; it is a threat to the stability of the planet. It is the determination of the strong to maintain their position by whatever means necessary, whether military, financial, or political, that is the basis for the systemic inequality in the world. A commitment to equity in the world is the only secure foundation for a more humane world order. Nations must work together to blunt current disparities and improve global stability. A continuation of the unjust status quo will inevitably lead to massive conflicts in the decades ahead.

An Equitable United Nations

In practical terms, changing the composition of the U.N. Security Council would have a profound effect on promoting equitability in the world and restoring confidence in the institution. Five countries, the United States, Russia, the United Kingdom, France, and China, have a permanent seat on the Security Council. Ten other seats are occupied by other States on a rotating basis, each for a two-year term. The permanent members each have a veto over any resolution; the nonpermanent members do not.

The make-up of the Security Council reflects the world that existed at the conclusion of World War II, with the Western States in the ascendancy. Much of Asia, Africa, and Central America were still colonies. The major powers, aware that they would be out-numbered in the General Assembly where each country has one vote, said that if they did not possess a veto in the Security Council, they would not join. Today, the permanent members represent only some 29 percent of world population; without the People's Republic of China that figure is drastically reduced to less than 10 percent. The entire continents of Africa and South America do not possess a permanent seat, and Asia, with half the population of the world, has only one. The veto power, possessed by the strongest, has become an anachronism in a time of spreading democracy. While the world should seek deeper integration and cooperation, the veto reflects domestic political agendas that are an affront to internationalism.

Why should the West, which Russia has joined in economic terms, possess four of the five permanent seats? Do the peoples of Africa, South and Central America, and Asia not count in the political determination of how peace and security will be obtained? By what right do the permanent members exercise a veto over what other countries, constituting a majority of world population, want to do? Other than their military might signaled by the possession of nuclear weapons, none. There can be little wonder both India and Pakistan felt the need to acquire weapons of mass destruction. Their nuclear testing, so disheartening since it occurred when the end of the nuclear age was thought to be at hand, underscores the need for U.N. Security Council reform.

For several years, reform of the U.N. has been debated. When the Western powers agreed that Germany and Japan could be admitted as permanent members, developing countries objected. When then asked to select one each from Latin America, Africa, and Asia to be added to the permanent list, they could not agree. The addition of more nonpermanent members is currently looked on as a way out of this dilemma.

U.N. reform of administrative issues has proceeded, but the biggest roadblock to achieving equity in power structures remains. If the U.N. is to regain its proper place as the guarantor of peace and security, this anomaly must be corrected. It is not likely that those who possess the veto power will give it up. But a modified veto, in which it would be necessary for three States to cast a veto for it to be effective, is possible. The determination of like-minded States to press the case for this substantive reform may prove effective. The major powers are not impervious to the views of other important States. But the latter must work together.

Law of the Jungle Weakens All

The struggle for equitable representation on the Security Council illustrates how international inequality remains a deeply entrenched and powerful force. In fact, the powerful continue to blatantly coerce the less powerful and simply trample on the weak. The weak, who need the benefits a new international economic order would bring, have no hope of attaining one. A "level playing field" is talked about but never developed. The markets of the globalized economies have soared while the weak struggle in the backwash.

Whether in environmental, international trade, or finance policies, poor countries lack both the technical and financial ability to pursue their own interests. Market globalism based on high technology available mainly to the rich has worsened inequities. While cries for equity and justice are not entirely unheard, they do not figure prominently in international discussions and negotiations. Self-interest remains the dominant language of bargaining power.

The confluence of the technological capacity for mutual destruction and the new acceptance of universal human rights—an entirely new phenomenon that infuses this moment in history with a powerful potential for creating a world order of more equity—should encourage nations to use their self-interest in an enlightened manner. A more equitable manner of the use of the world's goods would lay a stronger base for peace, trade, and prosperity. It is the job of true leadership to convince a society to forego immediate gains in exchange for the promise of future benefits. Leaving aside for the moment the dearth of true leadership today, it must be recognized that the old law of the jungle, which predominated in the past two colonial and industrial centuries, is the greatest obstacle to international cooperation. Today, it not only compromises the fairness needed in the development of all peoples but also jeopardizes the very survival of life on the planet.

Reciprocity, mutual concern, fair play, and justice must now be accorded a higher level of recognition and motivation in modern discourse. The search for global standards, based on equity, would be an enlightened act by governments. They would, in fact, be carrying out their duty to promote the right to development. Just as the state has been the pre-eminent instrument of coercion in society, it has the potential to be a powerful instrument of equity, justice, and efficiency. A global negotiating forum with broad representation could reconcile conflicting demands by allowing redistribution bargains. Developing countries' enforcement of tighter environmental regulations in return for debt cancellation measures is an example of such a bargain.

These ideas, stemming from the recognition of human rights, bring the notion of international solidarity into focus. Social cohesion that is today so noticeably absent in the market rush to globalization would contribute not only to lessening the fissures among people but also the binding of the international community. Even the willingness to attempt to find meaningful and equitable solutions to world problems can itself foster social and political co-operation.

The longer the delay in strengthening international institutions and rules to meet emerging challenges, the more market forces will worsen present inequities. In this sense, globalization is a challenge to democracy, as its guiding principles undermine democratic values where governments, promoting narrow private interests, are ceding their responsibility to the market ideology of a few at the expense of a wider public welfare. This ideology both accepts and in fact fosters strong inequalities among economic agents, whereas the political rights in a democracy are premised upon the equal rights of the citizenry. The free market concentrates power within nations and between them, and deprives many people of an ability to meet their basic economic rights and needs, leaving them less able to exercise their full political rights. If the marginalized are not included in global integration, continued instability in world systems will weaken the world community—by how much is yet to be determined.

The criteria of equity, legitimacy, and democracy are not only important means to effect co-operation but valuable ends in themselves. A time when nations practice enlightened self-interest may not yet have arrived, but the demand to end human inequalities is increasing.

The Role of Women in Peace

National inequalities are today better understood because of the rising demand to stamp out worldwide individual inequalities. In the development of a culture of human rights, no area offers such promise in building an equitable social order as promoting the rights of women. Over the past half-century the international community has expanded the interpretation of human rights in response to global developments, but only recently have such efforts addressed gender. The deleterious impact of gender discrimination and violence on the prospects of peace and development are most severe.

Although women constitute a majority of the world's population, there is still no society in which women enjoy full equality with men. In 1996, for example, women held only 7 percent of ministerial-level posts in governments worldwide. The exclusion of women from the benefits of economic activity and development are widespread globally. Even in our own society in Canada, the gender dimension has become critical, since many women are significantly over-represented in the new and precarious sectors of casual, part-time, and short-contract employment. The generally lower income level for women and their preponderance as the head of single-parent households is inexorably linked to the growing problem of child poverty.

As victims of violence and discrimination are chosen because of their gender, it is imperative that seeking redress must be a widely accepted goal in the advancement of human rights. According to UNICEF, violence against women and girls is the most pervasive violation of human rights in the world today. Cutting across economic, social, cultural, and religious barriers, violence against women is an insidious phenomenon affecting the lives of millions of women. A World Bank study found that, worldwide, 25 to 50 percent of all women suffer abuse by their partner. In virtually all armed conflict, rape is used as a cynical tactic to subjugate and terrify entire communities. Trafficking in women and girls, within and across borders, has reached alarming proportions. An estimated two million girls in at least 28 countries are subjected to the traumatizing traditional practice of female genital mutilation. In some societies, girls are compelled to marry at an early age before they are physically, mentally, or emotionally mature. Countless female embryos are aborted because of son-preference.

It is cynical to dismiss the degradation of females as an individual or cultural matter. Sexism kills; the World Health Organization reports that girls are fed less, breast fed for shorter periods of time, and die or are physically and mentally maimed by malnutrition at higher rates than males.

The international community did not take concrete action against the alarming global dimensions of gender-based violence until 1993, when the U.N. General Assembly adopted the Declaration on the Elimination of Violence Against Women. Until that point, most governments tended to regard violence against women largely as a private matter between individuals; and not as a pervasive human rights problem requiring active state intervention. The declaration, dealing with violence in the family, violence within the community, and violence perpetrated or condoned by the state, included in its definition of violence: systematic rape, sexual slavery, and forced pregnancy of women in situations of armed conflicts as extremely grave violations of the fundamental principles of human rights and international humanitarian law.

The U.N. is committed to combating violence against women by addressing the root causes of the problem and changing society's attitudes and mentality towards women. Information campaigns emphasizing the equal rights of women are directed to judges and police officers. Educating males to view women as equal partners in private and public life is crucial to fully democratizing society. The 1993 World Conference on Human Rights urged all governments and the U.N. system to work together towards banning all forms of sexual harassment and exploitation.

Women's movements have become instrumental in widening the horizons of not only women's rights, but also the potential for women to strengthen society. With increasing persuasiveness, women's groups have advocated that there are no human rights without women's rights, thus grounding the promotion and protection of the rights of women in the universality and indivisibility of all human rights.

This new emphasis was the cross-cutting theme of the Fourth World Conference on Women in Beijing in 1995. Attended by nearly 50,000 participants, the Beijing Conference on Women significantly strengthened the empowerment of women by elaborating the crucial links between the universal advancement of women and social progress around the world. The Beijing Declaration and Platform for Action advanced a number of forward-looking strategies to integrate a gender perspective and enhance women's participation in political, civil, economic, social, and cultural life. It went further than any previous document to set out an agenda for women's empowerment. The Platform for Action was based on the principle of shared power and responsibility between men and women at home, in the workplace, and in the wider national and international communities. Equality between men and women is a precondition for peace and people-centred sustainable development.

Women at Beijing stated that they wanted to play a greater role in decision-making, conflict prevention and resolution, and other peace initiatives to build the conditions for lasting peace. In the past, women have at various times in history played a pivotal role for peace. It was mothers in Europe, protesting against the presence of Strontium 90 in their breast milk as a result of radiation fallout from atmospheric nuclear testing that led to the 1963 Partial Test Ban Treaty, which shut off atmospheric tests. Women have formed an important nucleus in peace groups. But, women have not been the strong influence that one might have expected.

It is true that women have a hard time breaking through the "glass ceiling" that keeps many out of top jobs. But it is also true that the voice of women calling the predominantly male establishment to task for the perpetuation of the war machine and the double standards by which militarism is funded and social development starved is almost muted. Is this because there really is no significant difference between men and women's assessments of how to build peace and security, and that the received wisdom of the ages that women have a more nurturing character making them more peaceful is not true? Whatever the socially recognized differences between men and women, headed foremost by their respective biologies, I am left with the political wish that women in greater numbers would play a much more important role in ensuring that public policy becomes more human rights oriented.

Obviously, such a powerful event as the Beijing Conference will have a lasting effect as its programs influence women's and human rights movements around the world. The urgency of turning government policies away from the preparation for war and towards building the conditions for peace challenges women particularly to set their stamp on the 21st century.

The development of human rights is not just to protect the individual—man or woman. It also enables a rights-based approach to peace-building. The full application of human rights forges vital links between peace, democracy, and sustainable development. Strengthening respect for human rights and applying this to the agenda for peace and development will build a climate of confidence that can help society reach a sorely needed equilibrium.

Justice
Both Legal and Social

7

The development of international law is still at primitive levels.

No local community would allow two neighbours to fill their houses with explosives and ammunition and train their guns on each other. Yet that is how we live globally. A local authority can enforce a fine on you for running a red light. But there is no global authority to stop a polluter from interfering with the ozone layer and allowing the sun's rays to produce multiple skin cancers. The laws we take for granted at the domestic level are only now coming into shape in the international community.

An agenda for justice—legal and social—needs to be advanced by a world increasingly bewildered by trans-national environmental and humanitarian dilemmas. The agenda has been identified, but it is far from being implemented.

When the Declaration on the Fiftieth Anniversary of the United Nations reached the justice section, governments pledged respect for the rule of law. Governments said they would promote full respect for and implementation of international law. They would settle international disputes by peaceful means; they would ensure compliance with the obligations of international treaties; they would promote the progressive development of international law in the field of development, including those which would foster economic and social progress.

None of that has been done. The major powers have ignored their obligations under the Non-Proliferation Treaty; in the bombing of Serbia, Kosovo, and Iraq, NATO violated international law as set down by the U.N. Charter; nations have confined their commitment to establishing a legal basis for human development to rhetoric.

It is true that courts dealing with those who have committed war crimes are coming into existence, but a system of world law is still on the horizon. Nations are afraid that the enforcement of such a system would lead to a world government, a subject that is still taboo in an age when nation states still insist that their national sovereignty must be protected at all costs. As the 21st century develops or as the 22nd century dawns, it is unlikely that the authorities of that future period will continue to reject the idea of a world legal authority. By that time, the scale of environment, armaments, and poverty problems, already so dominant on today's agenda, will be so large and so obviously trans-national in scope that it will become conventional wisdom for humans to protect one another and the planet with an authority to enforce global laws. Such a step will be deemed to be "enlightened self-interest."

Defenders of national sovereignty today want to head off any such development and conjure up the spectre of world government as a threat. Hence, they block proposals for a world legal authority and a strengthened United Nations. A world legal authority does not require, or even imply, a world government; it could be managed by the U.N. Security Council, composed of an equitable distribution of permanent seats and devoid of individual veto power. Since changing the character of the Security Council is a long process, the development of international law, so urgently needed as the turmoil of the 1990s has revealed, is proceeding with the continued handicap of the supremacy of the nation state.

The excessive claims of the nation state restrict the ability of the International Court of Justice (ICJ) from enforcing its own decisions. The ICJ is actually the highest legal authority in the world, but it is deliberately kept in the background by the major States.

The ICJ, also known as the World Court, was established at The Hague in 1946 under a statute that is an integral part of the United Nations Charter. Composed of 15 elected judges who each serve a nine-year term, the Court has a dual role: to settle in accordance with international law the legal disputes submitted to it by States, and to give advisory opinions on legal questions referred to it by duly authorized international agencies. There is a catch: the Court's decisions on disputes are mandatory only when the parties have previously agreed to be so bound. Advisory opinions may possess wisdom and prestige, but they are not enforceable. Thus when Nicaragua took the U.S. to the World Court on the issue of mining the harbours of Nicaragua, the U.S. refused to accept the decision of the Court (which was in Nicaragua's favour). The 1996 advisory opinion of the Court on the legality of nuclear weapons and the Court's admonition that negotiations leading to nuclear weapons elimination must be concluded have simply been ignored by the Western NWS.

The World Court, then, which is neither a legislative body nor an academic institution, dispenses justice within the limits that have been assigned to it. There is no other judicial organ in the world that has the same capacity for dealing with the problems of the international community as a whole and offers States so wide a range of opportunities for promoting the rule of law. From 1946 to 1996, the Court dealt with 47 contentious cases and gave 23 advisory opinions. The Court's decisions provided a legal basis for decolonization, the Law of the Sea, the protection of foreign investments, and helped to bring into force the Vienna Convention on the Law of Treaties. Its advisory opinions have dealt with voting procedures, interpretation of peace treaties, and admission to U.N. membership. Handicapped as it is, the World Court plays a vital role in contributing to the development of international law.

The supreme court of any country can enforce its decisions; the World Court cannot. Though this anomaly reflects the continuing power of the nation state, the Court's contribution to the elevation of legal thinking has had tangible effects. The inauguration of courts to try war criminals came about as the result of public acceptance and demand for an international system to punish perpetrators of war crimes.

Most perpetrators of war crimes and crimes against humanity throughout history have gone unpunished. Although the Nuremberg Tribunal dealt with World War II criminals, perpetrators of atrocities in recent decades believed their crimes would go unpunished. There have been many instances of crimes against humanity committed in wars for which no individuals have been held accountable. In Cambodia in the 1970s, for example, the Khmer Rouge killed one million people. In many countries around the world, massacres of civilians, including countless women and children, continue to this day. In ethnic conflict, violence begets further violence; one slaughter is the parent of the next. The absence of a guarantee that at least some perpetrators of war crimes or genocide may be brought to justice stimulates future aggressors. The atrocities that occurred in the former Yugoslavia and Rwanda were widely seen as failures of the international community to intervene in time to prevent gross violations of human rights.

New Criminal Courts

Building on a number of conventions adopted over previous decades, the U.N. Security Council responded to the "ethnic cleansing" in the Yugoslav conflict between the Muslim, Serb, and Croatian communities by setting up the International Tribunal for the Prosecution of Persons Responsible for Serious Violations of International Humanitarian Law Committed in the Territory of the Former Yugoslavia Since 1991. The Tribunal, situated in The Hague, was given the broadest mandate of any international investigative body since the Nuremberg trials following World War II. Because the Tribunal was established under Chapter VII of the U.N. Charter, the Security Council can use sanctions and other measures to enforce the Tribunal's decisions.

The Tribunal holds trials and appellate proceedings on a regular basis, and its decisions make substantive findings on myriad legal issues, most of which have never before been considered by a court, or which have not been subject to legal review for decades. Examples are the applicability and scope of the Geneva and Genocide Conventions and the laws and customs of war, the responsibility of military and civilian authorities in time of conflict and definitions of armed conflict, war crimes, and the crime of rape. An essential element of the Tribunal's performance is its impact on international relations. In interpreting dormant treaties and actually applying international humanitarian law, the Tribunal is now developing that law. Since its establishment six years ago, the Tribunal has publicly indicted 89 individuals.

The Tribunal has primacy over national jurisdictions and can issue an international arrest warrant, as occurred in the case of Slobodan Milosevic, even if national authorities are unwilling to cooperate. While the Tribunal is hampered by an inability to get all those indicted into court, it has made a breakthrough because it has the right to find and try war criminals.

The Yugoslav Tribunal was followed a year later by a similar creation of the Rwanda Tribunal. In Rwanda, civil strife and internal violence led to genocide on a vast scale. A systematically planned genocide by extremist Hutu militia claimed the lives of at least 500,000 people. The main victims of this carnage were members of the Tutsi minority and moderate Hutus. The civil war forced hundreds of thousands of Rwandans to flee to neighbouring countries.

The Rwanda Tribunal, based in Arusha, Tanzania, started trials in 1998. So far the Tribunal, now composed of three Trial Chambers, an Appeals Chamber, a Prosecutor, and a Registry, is holding 36 people including former key personalities in Rwandan society and politics, and has already handed down life sentences to two people and sentenced one to 15 years' imprisonment.

Among the key personalities awaiting trials are nine former ministers and three cabinet directors, five high-ranking army officers, mayors, party leaders, businessmen, and professionals.

One of the most dramatic cases so far before the Tribunal has been the trial of Rwanda ex-Prime Minister Jean Kambanda, who pleaded guilty to genocide and was sentenced to life in prison. This was the first time in history that an accused individual publicly confessed to the crime of genocide. The judgement, according to U.N. Secretary-General Annan, is testament to the collective determination to confront the heinous crime of genocide in a way the international community never has before. It is a defining example of the ability of the United Nations to establish an effective international legal order and the rule of law.

The Yugoslav and Rwanda Tribunals stimulated the creation in 1998 of the International Criminal Court (ICC), with power to exercise its jurisdiction over persons anywhere for the most serious crimes of international concern. The development of the ICC has a long history. For nearly half a century, the U.N. has recognized the need to establish a Criminal Court to prosecute and punish persons responsible for crimes such as genocide. The International Law Commission worked for most of the 1990s to devise the architecture for a system of law that would complement national criminal courts, which would normally try alleged criminals within their jurisdiction. The International Court is needed only when national institutions have collapsed due to conflict (as in Rwanda) or when a state is unwilling to try its own nationals (as in the former Yugoslavia).

The ICC was finally created at a 1998 international conference in Rome, attended by delegations from 160 countries and 124 nongovernmental organizations. The Court was adopted by a vote of 120 in favor to 7 against, with 21 abstentions. The seven opponents were the United States, India, China, Israel, Bahrain, Qatar and Vietnam. The United States is clearly the most important and unfortunate absentee from the list of signatories because of its pre-eminent leadership role. With the largest number of troops serving overseas, the U.S. did not accept the concept of jurisdiction in the Statute of Rome. Fearing the possibility its soldiers might ever be brought to trial, its tough stance and aggressive diplomacy sought to make the Court's investigations dependent on the approval of the U.N. Security Council. That no national could be brought before the Court without the country's permission would have politicized everything the court did, seriously undermining its credibility and integrity.

The treaty establishing the Court needs to be ratified by at least 60 States before entering into force. When it begins functioning, the Court, operating with 18 judges situated in The Hague, will act on the principle of individual responsibility, applied equally and without exception to any individual throughout a government or military chain of command. The appropriate punishment would apply to heads of state and commanding officers as well as to low-ranking soldiers in the field.

The Court has weaknesses. For example, aggression in the making of war is not yet included in the specified crimes against humanity, which number a long list of offences on political, racial, national, ethnic, cultural, religious, and gender grounds. The crime of aggression will only be part of the Court's jurisdiction after a definition—sufficiently precise to meet the high level of specificity required of criminal law—has been determined. Nor are the use or threat of use of nuclear weapons, landmines, blinding laser weapons, or other weapons of mass destruction included in the Court's definition of war crimes, even though such weapons are inherently indiscriminate. The NWS made sure nuclear weapons would be excluded.

Still, with these deficiencies, and bearing in mind how difficult it is to get the international community to agree on controversial subjects, the creation of a permanent, wide-sweeping International Criminal Court is a giant step in the history of humanity. It fills in the missing link in the international legal system. The International Court of Justice handles only cases between States; the International Criminal Court will deal with individuals.

Since the ICC will have mandatory jurisdiction in enforcing its decisions, does it not follow that the ICJ too should have mandatory jurisdiction? Must individuals be forced to adhere to international law and be punished for gross violations while nation states can choose which aspects of international law they will accept or reject? Since the rights of the nation state are certainly not greater than the rights of the individual, there is no moral base for a nation state to hold itself superior to the requirements of international law. This is especially true in an era when the requirements of the human security agenda demand international management and cooperation.

The problem of how to compel States to follow international law remains a huge obstacle in building the conditions for peace. Power still triumphs over principle. That sad comment, though depressing when viewed in the short run, gives way to a measure of optimism when viewed in the long run. Nations, no matter how powerful, no longer have unfettered power to do what they want. The development of an international political structure, starting with the United Nations and its ancillary bodies and running through a host of regional groupings, has already had an effect on all countries and made them realize they are part of a world community. The European Union is an example of this national outreach. Modern technology, with its communications and information components, has contributed to a gradual elevation of understanding about human unity. The momentum of history is making States realize their inter-dependence. A binding law for common survival is the inevitable result of political enlightenment. Enlightenment dawns slowly on the most obdurate, to be sure. But not even the most powerful can stop the dawn from breaking.

From Legal to Social Justice

With individual human rights having opened up such a strong base for legal justice, a new framework for social justice has also been created. It used to be that social justice–treating human beings equitably–was viewed as an extension of the Sunday sermon. This is not to diminish the Sermon on the Mount or other spiritual admonitions, which provide a framework for correct human interaction in which the poor and vulnerable would receive their just desserts. The moral base for human compassion remains a powerful motivator. Concepts of redress for the needy have customarily been expressed in terms of charity. But today, as the result of the new understanding of human rights, and indeed the very right to development, the corollary of justice replaces charity in the claims of the poor on the rich.

Since the development of an international legal justice system is so difficult, we can appreciate how much harder it will be codifying social justice principles. I do not exclude that this can happen when the world has evolved into a higher level of civilization, a maturation process that any look-back into history will confirm is actually underway. Just as there is a legally provided social net, access to health and education, pensions for citizens of many countries, so too, in the name of social justice based on human rights for everyone, a floor can be provided globally to meet basic human needs.

In order for this to happen, more public understanding is needed about how the structures and mechanisms of modern society discriminate against the development of vulnerable peoples.

The crisis of today's disparities has its roots in the models of development and colonization that presumed development was a never-ending process of domination of the earth by the strong. The grasp of the market and of business characterized development for the past two centuries; the needs of the earth and its inhabitants were relegated to marginal considerations.

In modern times, the negative results of top-down development models, such as pollution, resource depletion, and the loss of species, have entered economic calculations. Yet, even with the new knowledge of the adverse effects of exponential economic development, great social and ecological deficits are left unattended. The demands of corporations and investors for fewer restrictions on trade and business have weakened environmental regulations. This immense financial power of major corporations has enabled them to ward off the imposition of corrective mechanisms. The same economic model that is injuring the earth is also impoverishing a majority of its inhabitants. Landlessness, ecological degradation, the concentration of wealth, the ravages of war, and the residue of colonization have created crushing poverty, hunger, and marginalization.

The past few years have brought increasing economic turbulence, widening social inequalities, and widespread feelings of insecurity and helplessness. The latest sign of the times is the outbreak of the East Asian financial crisis. Nations that were hailed as economic miracles have had their currencies depreciated and millions thrown out of work. The countries affected blame currency speculators. Avoiding any responsibility, the G8 nations and the International Monetary Fund instead blamed the affected countries for having the wrong policies and economic structures. As part of the conditions for the rescue packages for Thailand, Indonesia, and South Korea, they insisted that governments slash their budgets, raise interest rates, remove subsidies for essential items, and demanded reforms that enabled foreign companies to enter and accumulate new assets.

In short, developing countries are no longer able to control their own currencies and financial systems. The destabilization this causes is undermining their trade, investment, and development prospects. Structural adjustment programs, drawn up by the Western-controlled international financial institutions, and imposed on 80 or more indebted countries, have forced the poorest countries to repay the international banks at the cost of increased poverty, unemployment, social ills, and conflicts.

For several years, a nongovernmental forum, The Other Economic Summit (TOES), also known as the "People's Summit," has held a public meeting in conjunction with the annual G8 Summit to advocate a more just and sustainable society, "an economics as if people mattered." The People's Summit promotes economics that incorporate the sustainable use of natural resources and the productive engagement of all people in the development of their communities. This struggle to advance a social justice agenda does not get much public attention. But it is on the right track because the present economic system is demonstrably failing to provide for people.

Social justice demands changing the power structures, which have failed to meet the needs of the most vulnerable people. This requires foremost a change in the policies of the international financial institutions through democratic consultation with civil society and governments. The practical results might well include:

- The inauguration of the Tobin tax.

- A moratorium on environmentally and socially destructive projects.

- Cancellation of crushing debt burdens of developing countries.

- A halt to structural adjustment programs that deepen poverty.

- Ending the piles of military weapons and putting more resources into the peaceful settlement of disputes.

A social justice agenda is being written today by caring people. Electing caring governments prepared to implement such an agenda is the next step.

Social Justice
A Daily Struggle

Canada: The U.N. and/or NATO?

8

The Kosovo crisis of 1999 exposed the contradictions in Canadian foreign policy.

For a long time, Canada has tried to balance its adherence to the United Nations system and its allegiance to NATO. When the U.N. was trying to rid the world of nuclear weapons and NATO said they were essential, Canada tried to accommodate both viewpoints. When NATO expanded into Eastern Europe at the expense of the development of the pan-European security body, the Organization for Security and Cooperation in Europe, Canada went along. When the United States and the U.K. began, in 1998, protracted bombing of Iraq without any mandate from the U.N. Security Council, Canada acceded.

The war opened up by NATO's bombing of Serbia and Kosovo in direct violation of the U.N. Charter, as well as NATO's own Charter, has brought the fissures between Western military might and the global strategies of the United Nations into the open. Canada is still trying to balance its adherence to both the U.N. and NATO. Increasingly, this is becoming an impossible task as the differences between each become irreconcilable. The U.N. wants peace through international consensus and law. NATO wants peace through over-riding international consensus and law.

Canada is caught in a dilemma. Its fundamental values lie with the United Nations as the guarantor of international peace and security. Its own protection during the Cold War lay with a Western military alliance that would come to Canada's defence if attacked. As long as there was a reasonable compatibility between the two, Canada could absorb the clashing of the two systems.

In choosing to not only support but participate in NATO's bombing of Serbia and Kosovo, Canada—for the moment—put NATO above the U.N. Of course the other NATO members did the same thing; they all subverted international law by war. The pragmatics of attempting to stop the ethnic cleansing and atrocities suffered by the Kosovars at the hands of the Serbs won out over the principle that only the U.N. Security Council has the right to take military action against an aggressor.

The Kosovo crisis points to an inescapable fact: the world must avoid such future conflicts to head off a global war. The former Soviet leader, Mikhail Gorbachev, warned that the views of other major countries, such as Russia, China, and India, must be taken into account. Air strikes by a powerful Western alliance are an affront to these other major nations. They are not going to sit quietly by while a powerful, nuclear-armed Western alliance asserts its dominance.

Canada, which lobbied hard for its present role on the Security Council, is instrumentally placed to press for the implementation of a viable and effective United Nations system. This means the reassertion of the predominant responsibility of the U.N. Security Council as the guarantor of peace and security in the world.

If the post-Cold War period had not been rocked by one crisis after another (the Gulf War, Somalia, Rwanda, Yugoslavia), the international system might have been able to evolve more harmoniously into agreed mechanisms for peace. But throughout the chaotic 1990s, NATO became stronger and the United Nations weaker. This was just the reverse of what was needed to build a foundation for peace supportable by all the regions of the world. Instead of strengthening a newly democratic Russia in an integrated Europe with actions, not just rhetoric, the West promoted the expansion of NATO, which Russia interpreted as a threat. Instead of reducing significantly unneeded armaments in Europe, and joining in mounting world opinion that nuclear weapons must be eliminated because they are too dangerous for all, NATO, dominated by the U.S., flaunted a vast military might. The U.S. share of global military spending increased from 30 percent to 34 percent, and with its NATO allies, Japan and South Korea, far outspent the rest of the world combined. The U.N., meanwhile, was put in the shadows by under-financing and major power refusal to provide the U.N. with a permanent peace-making force capable of rapid deployment. The total cost of all U.N. peacekeeping operations in 1997 was some $1.3 billion–the equivalent of less than 0.5 percent of the U.S. military budget, and less than 0.2 percent of global military spending.

How would such awesome military power ever be used in response to the challenges now facing the contemporary international system, such as wealth and resource distribution disparities, ethnic, religious, and cultural strife? Militarization over peacemaking has been building up for some time. Is the Kosovo solution to aggression, with its overwhelming military force at the expense of effective diplomacy, now to be the standard on the false assumption that the U.N. is too weak to act? Canada clearly hopes not. And Canada will doubtless work to strengthen the U.N. The question, opened up by Kosovo, is: Can Canada work effectively with both, if NATO continues to override U.N. operations? Should Canada leave NATO if the alliance continues to demonstrate that it is primarily an instrument of U.S. foreign policy?

Answers to these questions will gravely affect the conduct of Canada's future foreign policy. The answers can only be found by looking deeply into ourselves; far more than the powerful weight of the United States is involved in defining who we are as Canadians in the new multilateral world.

A Sparkling Image No More

The record of Canada's contributions to peace and security in the world is a long one. Starting in the "Golden Age" of Canadian foreign policy in the 1940s and 1950s, a period that saw Lester B. Pearson win a Nobel Peace Prize for instigating U.N. peacekeeping, Canada has worked steadfastly to advance specific themes. Canada's commitment to peacekeeping missions is justly celebrated and was a strong component of the U.N.'s overall peacekeeping effort, which was also awarded a Nobel Peace Prize in 1998. Through scientific and diplomatic work, Canada has promoted verification techniques as an essential prerequisite to meaningful disarmament. Canada has done the spadework to enable the U.N. —if there is ever political agreement—to establish a rapid reaction force of 5,000 military and civilian personnel to be deployed by the Security Council to crisis areas. Canada was the chief promoter and organizer of the Anti-Personnel Landmines Treaty, overcoming skeptics who said such a treaty could never be achieved. Canada played a leading role in the development of the International Criminal Court. Canada removed its armed forces personnel from Europe soon after the end of the Cold War, despite NATO's displeasure. And Canada was a leading strategist in securing the indefinite extension of the Non-Proliferation Treaty in 1995.

All these measures have given Canada a well-earned international reputation. The names of outstanding Canadians who have served in international posts add further lustre: Bill Barton, Yvon Beaulne, Alan Beesley, Margaret Catley-Carlson, Brock Chisholm, Elizabeth Dowdswell, Dick Foran, Yves Fortier, Louise Frechette, King Gordon, John Holmes, John Humphrey, George Ignatieff, Hugh Keenleyside, Tamar Oppenheimer, Geoffrey Pearson, Saul Rae, Adelaide Sinclair, Maurice Strong. Canada, the thirty-second most populous country in the world, is the eighth largest financial supporter of the U.N. system.* So

---

* The budgeted top eight contributors are the USA (25%); Japan (15.4%); Germany (9%); France (6.4%); the U.K. (5.3%); Italy (5.2%); Russia (4.5%); Canada (3.1%). Collectively, they account for more than 73% of the regular U.N. budget.

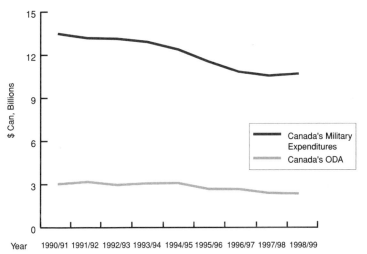

**Canadian Military Expenditures vs.
Canadian Official Development Assistance**

Year — 1990/91 1991/92 1992/93 1993/94 1994/95 1995/96 1996/97 1997/98 1998/99

Note: ODA figure for 1997/98 is an estimate; ODA figure for 1998/99 is a projection.
Sources: CIDA, Canadian Historical ODA System, Project Ploughshares.

closely imaged is Canada at home and abroad with the U.N.,
that it is little wonder the Canadian government trumpets the
U.N.'s ranking of Canada as the number one country in the
world in terms of quality of life indices.

There are, however, inconsistent policies that consider-
ably detract from the image Canada has fostered. Canada's ODA
programs are in decline, but defence spending priorities remain
misplaced. In the 1990s, Canada's ODA was cut 37 percent; ODA
spending is at $2.045 billion. In this same period, Canada's
defence budget was cut 25 percent and now stands at $10.2
billion. Canada, with approximately 60,000 personnel in the
armed forces, professes to maintain a combat posture in three
spheres—air, land, and sea. This does little but maintain the
illusion of an effective fighting force. Canada's effectiveness in
building security would be greater by putting less resources into
combat readiness and more into addressing the sources of con-

flict. But during the first half of the 1990s, Canadian human security assistance to the 48 most vulnerable countries dropped by one-third.

With major procurement programs emphasizing equipment capable of high intensity combat, and shifting government spending away from preventive, nonmilitary security programs, Canada primarily prepares itself for war, not peace. Regrettably, the ODA that relieves the economic and environmental conditions that foster today's low-intensity conflicts and humanitarian disasters has been neglected. The long-term benefits of ODA and its potential to address the problems that lead to conflict would save scores of lives, facilitating the vision of more relevant military priorities and effective spending.

Canada has no reason to feel smug because it is a small player in the arms trade, since it exports arms to several countries involved in military conflict and human rights violations. Canadian military exports in the post-Cold War period have leveled off at just over $1 billion per year to some 67 countries.

Canada's performance in building up environmental protection standards has been abysmal. Canada has failed to deliver on its Rio Summit commitments, with greenhouse gas emissions continually above 1990 levels, and fossil fuel production having increased by some 30 percent. Government cutbacks at both the federal and provincial levels have severely hurt environmental protection programs and monitoring.

Canada's determination to export products of dubious merit, such as CANDU reactors and asbestos, ignoring the proven health and environmental risks, also detracts from our sparkling image.

The centerpiece of the ambiguities in Canadian foreign policy is the problem of nuclear weapons. Though it espouses ultimate elimination, Canada supports the present retention of nuclear weapons. Here the discrepancies between NATO and the U.N. are at their sharpest. U.N. resolutions have called for comprehensive negotiations leading to the elimination of nuclear weapons. The three Western NWS of NATO adamantly refuse. Non-nuclear members of NATO, such as Canada and Germany, that want movement on this issue, have to be content with a NATO announcement that a review will be started. It will take immense pressure against the NATO system just to get NATO to adopt a No-First-Use policy, let alone shun nuclear weapons entirely.

The very manner in which Canada articulates its nuclear weapons policies reveals the strictures felt in trying to serve two masters.

Canada states proudly that it does not possess nuclear weapons, works to prevent their proliferation, and wants to see their political significance devalued. Having said that, Canada continues to live under the nuclear umbrella of NATO, stays quiet when the U.S. reaffirms nuclear weapons at the heart of its military doctrine, and refuses to state that nuclear weapons have no moral or legal justification and should be completely stripped of political legitimacy.

Canada wants Russia and the U.S. to take their nuclear weapons off alert status to increase the margin of safety against unauthorized or accidental use of nuclear weapons, but refuses to denounce the First-Use policies of the NWS. Canada says it will work with the New Agenda Coalition in pursuing disarmament objectives, but refuses to support negotiations on a nuclear weapons disarmament convention. Canada calls for a new Statement of Principles and Objectives at the 2000 Review Conference on the Non-Proliferation Treaty, but stops short of protesting the violation of Article VI of the NPT by the NWS. Canada condemns India and Pakistan for joining the nuclear weapons club, but is mute on its NATO partners' possession of nuclear weapons.

The government readily admits it has to "balance" its nuclear disarmament goals and loyalty to NATO. At the heart of Canada's policy statement is this passage:

The Government agrees that Canada intensify its efforts to advance the global disarmament and non-proliferation regime.... The United Nations continues to be the key vehicle for pursuing Canada's global security objectives.... As an active member of NATO and a net contributor to overall Alliance Security, as a friend and neighbour of the United States and its partner in NORAD...Canada balances its Alliance obligations with its disarmament and non-proliferation goals.

There are glaring inconsistencies in these policies. This is not because Canada really cannot make up its mind. There is no doubt that latter day Canadian governments, left alone, would fully espouse the complete elimination of nuclear weapons now. But they are not left alone. The pressure from the U.S., abetted by the U.K. and France, to support Western retention of nuclear weapons is intense.

All through the Cold War, the U.S. Administration reminded Canada that the U.S. could not tolerate a neutral state on its long northern border; on security matters, Canada would have to follow the U.S. lead. During the Cold War, Canada recognized U.S. leadership. That is why former Prime Minister Pierre Trudeau agreed to test nuclear Cruise Missile delivery systems in Canadian airspace even though he wanted to resist.

In the post-Cold War years, the U.S. has maintained its dominance over Canada's security policies. The entangled nature of Canada's alliance with the U.S. is so complex that a strong body of opinion in Ottawa holds that it is not in Canada's economic interests to tangle with the U.S. The U.S. is too big, too strong; we are too small, too vulnerable. More than 80 percent of Canada's trade is with the U.S., some $1 billion a day. This cannot be jeopardized.

When Canada took an international initiative to ban landmines, the U.S. did not like it (and did not sign the eventual treaty), but did not protest too much since landmines are not central to U.S. military doctrine. But nuclear weapons are. Thus for Canada to formally request NATO to review its nuclear weapons policy was tantamount to challenging the longstanding U.S. determination that NATO maintain nuclear weapons. Canada's statements on nuclear weapons definitely fall short of the unambiguous stance it ought to take, but measured against the opposition by the U.S., which even protested against the mere holding of a review by the Parliamentary Committee on Foreign Affairs and International Trade, Canada has demonstrated a bit of bravery. By setting an example for other non-nuclear NATO States to follow, Canada is demonstrating some diplomatic dexterity. But this action, while laudable, is weak and not commensurate with the gravity of the problem of world security. Of course, Canada does not have the power to force the U.S.–or any other NWS–to give up its nuclear weapons. But by subordinating its quest for the development of international law that would be strong enough to enforce a ban on nuclear weapons, Canada's lukewarm statements amount to a tacit acceptance of the status quo.

The status quo–the continued possession of nuclear weapons by the five permanent members of the Security Council while proscribing their acquisition by any other nation–will not hold. The world must implement a total ban on nuclear weapons or witness their proliferation into several other countries. Canada, precisely because of its excellent credentials, is well placed to lead an international campaign to de-legitimize nuclear weapons. Canada cannot do this alone. It will only be effective through working with like-minded States so that a new coalition of respected middle-power States can together mount a kind of pressure on the NWS that they cannot–if they want to be regarded, as they do, as respectable nations themselves–disregard.

A "Soft Power" Agenda

The abolition of nuclear weapons fits perfectly into the human security agenda (advanced by a "soft power" approach) espoused so well for over two years by Canada's Foreign Minister, Lloyd Axworthy. This new agenda, recognizing that true human security results only from an approach that integrates disarmament, development, environmental protection, and human rights, depends on the power to co-opt, rather than coerce, others to the goal. It recognizes that military and economic power, while still important, do not have the overwhelming pre-eminence they once did. Instead, the ability to communicate, negotiate, mobilize opinion, work within multilateral bodies, and promote international initiatives is increasingly important. Brilliant use of the interplay of these tools, in what was known as the "Ottawa Process," achieved the Landmines Treaty. Powerful ideas rather than powerful weapons, public diplomacy rather than backroom bargaining, and a working partnership between like-minded governments and civil society all are part of the mix of soft power. The work that Canada does in fostering data collection and analysis for early warning, de-mining and protection of civilian populations, human rights training, mediation and negotiation, reintegration of refugees and psycho-social trauma counseling, electoral assistance and judicial reform and training, and the implementation of peace accords has undoubted value.

Soft power should not be misconstrued as softness. Minister Axworthy pointed out: "It is difficult to understand how dealing with the devastating impact of landmines, the proliferation of small arms, the scourge of drugs, the exploitation of children, preventive measures against war crimes—and organizing concrete global action to confront them—could be interpreted by some as a sign of weakness."

Soft power challenges the old equation that military equals strength. In fact, soft power can involve using strong measures, including sanctions and military force. These stern measures are included in the U.N. Charter—which is why a standing U.N. peace force is foreseen. Again, such a force, to have legitimacy conferred on it by international law, must operate under the mandate of the Security Council. Canada's refusal to challenge NATO's peremptory action in Kosovo and Serbia reveals that the evolution of soft power has not reached the point where it directly challenges the major Western States, which are themselves holding back the development of a world security regime supported by all regions.

If Canada does not carry its peace-building aspirations into the field of abolishing nuclear and other weapons of mass destruction, much of its efforts will be lost in the hardening of attitudes between the NWS and the non-nuclear nations currently corroding international relations. The international community is moving to new and higher levels of danger posed by a 21st century breakout from the Non-Proliferation Treaty. What Canada is doing in espousing soft power is praiseworthy but lamentably short of the actions needed to end the biggest dangers of all to human security.

What is really holding Canada back?

A series of roundtables conducted across Canada in 1998 by Project Ploughshares, an ecumenically based research organization specializing in disarmament and development, considered this question in depth. I participated in these discussions. The 384 community leaders who attended the two-and-a-half hour sessions felt that the ambiguity of Canada projecting itself as a peacekeeper (even a peacemaker) yet supporting NATO's nuclear stance undermines the integrity of our overall foreign policy. Some participants argued that Canada should withdraw from NATO if NATO's nuclear policies are not changed. Others were uncertain. There are mixed feelings in the public about whether Canada should be in NATO at all, a doubt that is bound to grow as a result of NATO's relentless bombing of Serbia and Kosovo. Many who have examined the dangers attached to the present nuclear weapons situation heavily favour getting nuclear weapons out of NATO and, if that cannot be done, getting Canada out of NATO.

The roundtable participants recognized that Canada, living under the U.S.-led nuclear umbrella, is virtually forced to support the U.S. in opposing comprehensive negotiations leading to the elimination of nuclear weapons. Or is it? The question of precisely why the Canadian government feels it has to go against its own instincts, and the wishes of the overwhelming majority of Canadians as shown in public opinion surveys, is intriguing, especially now that the strictures of the Cold War ought to have been lifted.

In what precise way would the U.S. retaliate against Canada for taking concrete steps towards the abolition of nuclear weapons? Perhaps an answer to that question was provided by the U.S. State Department, which suddenly, in 1999, removed Canada's favoured status as a defence and aerospace trading partner, a move that could put $5 billion a year worth of Canadian exports in jeopardy.

The U.S. government had earlier signaled that it did not want Canada tampering with NATO's nuclear weapons policies. In an unusual act for a diplomat to criticize his host country, U.S. Ambassador Gordon D. Giffin gave a speech in Montreal, stating that NATO's strategy had served Canada well and does not need changing; and that Canada should be spending more on defence. The meaning and import of this speech extended far beyond his two points. For throughout his address, Ambassador Giffin implied that Canada's interests are best served by going along with U.S. views on the further development of the North American defence partnership.

This was undoubtedly an attempt to soften Canadian opinion to accept the new national ballistic missile system on a fast track for development in the U.S. A missile defence system is inherently a bad idea because it stimulates an opponent to develop new offensive weapons; that is why the U.S. and the Soviet Union signed the Anti-Ballistic Missile Treaty in 1972. The end of the Cold War notwithstanding, the U.S. is forging ahead to develop a defence system against unknown enemies and inexorably drawing Canada into the web of the military-industrial complex. Ambassador Giffin's speech was a thinly veiled warning to Canada to stay on board U.S. military policy.

A Break With U.S. Nuclear Policy?

The cleavage between U.S. and Canadian views on foreign policy is becoming more evident. The U.S. has given several indications that the development of the international community through a process of law takes second place to the continued assertion of the primacy of U.S. power. U.S. rejection of the International Criminal Court, opposition to the Landmines Treaty, the undermining of the U.N. through refusal to pay dues in full, the rejection of the authority of the Security Council through bombing of Iraq, Sudan, Libya, Serbia, and Kosovo and the Senate's rejection of the Comprehensive Test Ban Treaty are all manifestations of an "America First" attitude. The U.S. has only 4.56 percent of world population, but the government, calling the U.S. the "indispensable" nation, tends to act as if its view should dominate world discussion and decide world problems.

The gravity of the nuclear non-proliferation crisis indicates that Canada may have to break with U.S. nuclear policy—if Canada is to be true to its principles. However, many Canadians place a higher value on a good relationship with the U.S. than on a more independent nuclear disarmament policy. Broader public debate in Canada is needed to address this question. At the moment, the government is not prepared to withstand U.S. displeasure should Canada repudiate the doctrine of nuclear deterrence by coming out squarely for immediate comprehensive negotiations leading to the elimination of nuclear weapons. The present concern of the government is to enhance, not diminish, our relationship with the United States. Canada will not openly reject U.S. nuclear policies unless compelled to by Canadian public opinion.

An Angus Reid poll of 1998 showed that 92 percent of Canadians, when asked a direct question, favour their government taking a leadership role in global negotiations to eliminate nuclear weapons. This is a weakly expressed opinion. The peace community writes a lot of letters into the Ottawa system, but in the day-to-day reports in the media, there is scarce mention of the dilemma of nuclear weapons.

If Canadians were more aggressive in expressing their views to the government, would that make a difference in government action? Would the government then be able to say to the U.S. that Canada had no choice, electorally speaking, but to take strong action? I believe the problem is deeper than merely laying Canada's ambiguities at the U.S. doorstep. It is not the U.S. that is responsible for Canada dropping its Official Development Assistance to a projected 0.26 percent of GNP, the lowest level of aid since the U.N. 0.7 percent of GNP target was set three decades ago. The U.S. is not responsible for Canada's weak environmental performance. There is instead a weakening of the Canadian will to play a leading role in advancing solutions to the great security problems of our time. This weakening of Canadian will plays into U.S. obduracy on nuclear weapons.

The planes that Canada sent to bomb Serbia and Kosovo illustrate the skewing of Canada's priorities. Canada sent the planes to show that it was an active participant in the NATO action; but their need, relative to the overwhelming U.S. strength, was marginal. Canada's effort to resolve the Kosovo crisis would have been better served by using resources to strengthen political and diplomatic endeavours, then contribute forces to a U.N. approved international force. This would have underscored Canada's commitment to international law, but it would have meant stepping outside of NATO's action.

Canada is not ready to leave NATO. Yet Canada wants U.N. solutions. So the country continues to try to balance both sets of obligations. It is becoming clearer that remaining in a nuclear-armed Western military alliance is undermining Canada's ability and desires to express our yearning for peace through the United Nations system. If, by remaining in NATO, Canada can successfully work with allies to eliminate NATO's reliance on nuclear weapons and ensure that NATO works under, not above, the U.N., the allegiance will be worthwhile.

But it will take far more determination than yet seen by Canadian government action to achieve these goals. As long as NATO remains imperious, the demand of thinking Canadians, concerned about the requirements for a truly global security system, for Canada to leave NATO will grow.

Media, Politics and the Corruption of Values

9

A national television network came to my office to interview me concerning the Canadian government's decision to consider converting excess plutonium from the United States and Russia's nuclear weapons into mixed oxide (MOX) fuel for Canada's nuclear reactors. "I need your response in a 12-second clip," said the interviewer.

In such situations, there is not much to be gained by sitting down the interviewer and explaining that this is a complex subject. It touches on dangers to the environment in Canada, the need to find secure storage facilities for nuclear plutonium, and how such action by Canada actually underwrites continued maintenance by the Nuclear Weapons States of their outrageously large strategic nuclear forces into the indefinite future.

Television is not particularly good at dealing with complexities. So I made a stab at saying something like: "It is a spurious argument that Canada would contribute to nuclear disarmament by using in our nuclear reactors excessive weapons fuel from the Nuclear Weapons States." (Was that 12 seconds?) The interviewer went away happy.

It is futile to blame all the sins of the world on the media, though politicians are sometimes wont to do this (perhaps to escape some of the heat for their own sins). It is equally futile to blame all the sins of the world on politicians, though the media frequently feel disposed to do so. Media and the political process together are responsible for a corruption of the public policy process that perpetuates the grossest disparities in which money is readily found for war but cannot be produced to enhance human security.

While media and politicians justly deserve rebuke for undermining human values, criticism should not stop there. The duplicity that characterizes modern society has its roots in the attitudes and actions of citizens themselves. This is particularly true of those who have, either through diligence or good fortune, reached the commanding heights of the worlds of commerce, education, religion, and the professions and thus are able to control and manipulate the god of public opinion. The media and politicians, in turn, defer to public opinion with all the reverence usually accorded citations from the bible.

Thus my criticism of the political hypocrisies that justify a political and economic system that spends countless sums on endless wars but cannot feed and put every child in the world into a classroom must strike at societal inertia that continues to tolerate such anomalies.

In trying to understand why society is the way it is, we must first look at the media. It is too powerful an influence in our daily life to be overlooked. The media comes in all sizes and shapes, so that various tastes can be accommodated, especially by reaching for specialized publications or tuning in particular channels. But the mainline media—the TV networks, the daily papers—increasingly reflect a dominant characteristic: corporate control. In Canada today, two corporations run by Conrad Black and Ken Thomson control nearly 70 percent of all daily newspapers with 55 percent of circulation. Television networks have a similar concentration of control, reflected in a global commercial media system dominated by a small number of super-powerful interests who have stakes in numerous industries and enterprises. Mainline media outlets in the United States, which impact so strongly on Canadian TV viewing, are increasingly coming under the wing of mega communications giants.

Journalists are quick to point out that their integrity should not be questioned just because they work for a corporation. Let us not, then, raise such questions. Rather, let us ask why business news is covered in such depth, with daily special sections, while editorial treatment of the social justice agenda (an agenda, I repeat, which provides the basis for human security) is relegated to the bottom or the back of newspapers and virtually ignored by telecasts? Why is war given so much space and time in the media but the creative work of building the conditions for peace treated like a curiosity? When war, confrontations, and natural disasters are not dominating the news, why are media resources devoted in such excessive amounts to the trivial, the scandalous, and the prurient?

To raise such questions is to challenge the corporate psychology that increasingly drives media. I am not referring here only to those outlets known as "infotainment," where entertainment has taken over hard news. I am rather pointing to the standard news outlets where editorial decisions are made daily on the effects, not the causes, of situations. Rarely does the mass media make the connection between hunger and its root causes of poverty and powerlessness. Issues like the persistence of massive military spending in the post-Cold War era are not examined. The public is concerned about jobs, hunger, homelessness, health care, education, and the environment, but the media mostly report on these issues in ways that reinforce, and not disturb, the existing economic and social system. Media exclude stories and viewpoints that challenge corporate power.

While information from a wide perspective is available from alternate sources, it is the mainline media, operating from a base of the status quo so heavily protected by advertisers who want to enlarge, not restrict, the consumerist appetite, that dominate public opinion. In short, the mass media determines the parameters of public debate.

The Western, business, consumerist model predominates in the mass media. While it is possible to challenge this—David

Suzuki is an outstanding example—most public commentators are chosen because they reinforce existing belief systems and value structures. Experts who explain the waging of war find a home in TV studios; experts in peaceful conflict resolution are rare visitors.

Two decades ago, UNESCO prompted a movement known as the "new world information order," that would foster the presentation of news from a more international than Western viewpoint. Developing countries said they were fed up with Western news organizations focussing only on failure, riots, and crime when reporting on developing countries and virtually ignoring success stories. Distorted images prejudiced Western publics, they believed, against the potential of the vast majority of humanity that lives in developing countries. Whereas more balanced news coverage of their development would favourably affect Western public opinion and thus encourage Western countries to be more open towards negotiating a new international economic order. The fury of Western news organizations, which smelled censorship, blew away the new world information order, but not before the U.S. and the U.K. departed from UNESCO in protest.

Governments in democracies will not challenge the "right" of news organizations to present and comment on the news as they see fit. Governments in totalitarian regimes that control the dissemination of news play into the hands of Western communications executives who want unbridled freedom.

We are left in the West with mainline media that, for profit motives above all else, dwell on the confrontational rather than the creative. All the nuances and inter-connections between disarmament, development, environmental protection, and human rights are given short shrift.

The Marketplace of Politics

Inevitably, the media's incessant depiction of a culture of confrontation and consumerism infuses the political system. Politics has become a marketplace reflecting the win-lose dominance of business thinking.

Most politicians are decent persons, neither more altruistic nor venal than the average person, though their ambition and ego levels are somewhat higher. They are taught upon entry into the political process, at whatever level, that power is the only important thing. "If you don't have power, you can't do anything," is the constant refrain. Getting power means beating the opposition. Leaving aside the new phenomenon of "attack ads," which have lately come to disgrace election campaigns, politicians are convinced they will get power by promising to bring more benefits to the voter by making the existing economic and social order work better.

Politicians play to the consumerist appetite in their quest for power. It is a rare politician who will stand up in an election campaign and declare that the people around him are contributing to the North-South divide by demanding even more of the resources of the world and that he/she, if elected, will actually work for a social justice agenda that will more equitably distribute the world's resources and wealth. It is almost a fantasy to consider that the nominee of a major party seeking office would so deliberately campaign against the prevailing culture. Some aspirants actually do so, but they represent splinter parties, or only themselves, and they are quickly marginalized. I ran and won in four federal election campaigns, and the number of times I was asked for my views on the over-arching themes of disarmament and development could be counted on the fingers of one hand. Foreign policy, as the pundits say, does not get into election campaigns.

The political process is dominated by the powerful elements of society who want, at the very least, to retain their power. Though ceilings for campaign donations and disclosure laws may be put in place (the political process wants to keep corruption from becoming absolute corruption), the bulk of campaign contributions come from corporations and the upper classes. The galas, the fund-raisers, and the special solicitations are all underwritten by business interests that want to influence political leaders. Business interests dominate the formulation of public policy. Of that, there is no doubt. When NATO held its fiftieth anniversary summit in Washington, D.C. in 1999, the giants of the corporate world chipped in to pay for the $8 million celebration; corporate sponsorship of the events making up the annual summit of the G8 has become standard.

Just as journalists do not want their personal integrity questioned because they work for corporations, so too politicians would recoil from any suggestion that they personally profit from their dependence on business support. Though corrupt politicians are unearthed from time to time, that is not my point here. I am concerned by the way of thinking that predominates in the political process, which assumes that peace will come through the application of military power and that the vulnerable people in society will be helped by the overall expansion of the economy, led by the smartest and strongest. "A rising tide lifts all boats."

The thinking that has predominated through two hundred years of the industrial age and the rise of modern technologies has produced a culture overwhelmingly self-centered. There has always been room for charity and, indeed, spectacular instances of humanitarian aid, whether at the personal or nation-state level, have occurred. But the constant aggressiveness of business and political interests has been the driving force of progress. There is scant room for social justice in this agenda.

The Great Issues Are Moral Issues

In this two hundred-year period, the myth has taken hold that morality cannot be legislated. The separation of church and state has led to a moral disorder in society. This is not because religion or the churches have all the answers to economic and social programs and need to be at the political table. Rather, the rigidities of classifying morality under the heading of religion have deprived the political process from questioning whether the perpetuation of a system built on greed is in the best long-term interests of society. The great questions of our time—peace, equitability, sustainable development—are moral questions. To attempt to resolve such issues without reference to morality is fatuous.

It is true that morality is sometimes cloaked in effusive spirituality, which is then interpreted by politicians as a "special interest," and thus discounted. The projection of a moral truth is rejected as oxymoronic. Religion, while accorded the lip services of a political blessing, is feared by those on the commanding heights of society.

From time to time, religious leaders are received by political decision-makers or they issue statements and declarations of concern. Once in a while, as occurred with the 1983 issuance by the Social Justice Commission of the Canadian Catholic Bishops Conference of their economic critique, "Ethical Reflections," they stir up the political pot. For the most part, religious leaders confine themselves to issuing admonitions to advance social justice issues. The faithful have within them coteries of activists, but the echo from the pews, for the most part, is hard to hear.

The overall influence of religion on politics is minimal. The infusion of values-based principles into public policy is then left to individuals working on their own either within or without the political system, or the occasional commission, such as the Commission on Global Governance. The Commission's emphasis that all humanity could agree on the core values of respect for life, liberty, justice and equity, mutual respect, caring, and integrity suggests that not much political thought has so far been devoted to establishing and reinforcing a common ground. Could the recognition of a universal moral community provide the basis for human security policies that mutually enrich every region of humanity?

Daily crises preoccupy the political agenda. These get the news attention. Underneath all the legitimate concerns of the moment is a human crisis which, in brief, revolves around how we are going to treat one another as brothers and sisters on one planet—where every aspect of life in one location is affected by the decisions and questions of another. It is a human crisis when millions of children die each year from malnutrition and water-borne diseases, but it is not news. It is a human crisis when wars take place in distant lands, but if CNN does not send cameras, it is not news. It is a human crisis when the powerful persist in flexing their power with nuclear weapons, but the media ignore this.

The social justice agenda I have outlined addresses the human crisis. In so doing, it contributes to the long-range benefit of all of humanity. That this is not yet something politicians would delight in loudly trumpeting is a result of the fence that still exists between morality and politics. The political system is thus left to talk of "balance" and "neutrality" when, in fact, the perpetuation of the status quo, no matter the degree of cosmetics in social legislation, reinforces moral disorder.

The discovery in the 1990s of the human security agenda is an important step forward in advancing social justice. The U.N. global conferences have produced a new understanding of interrelated issues such as environmental protection, the well-being of children, human rights and the rights of women, population, unemployment, crime, trade, food security, human settlements, natural disasters, and social cohesion. The U.N. has called for a common framework to express the linkages between all the security themes. Coherent strategies have been articulated. A common concept of development, centred on human beings, their needs, rights, and aspirations, is coming into view. Public grasp of the urgency of this integrated agenda for peace and human security is needed before we can expect governments to promote sustainable economic growth and an equitable system of multilateral cooperation.

Policies to solidify the common good express a morality. Why, then, shy away from espousing a social justice agenda based on the moral values of mutual respect, caring, and equity? Yet the media and politicians would generally consider this to be "idealistic" at best; they prefer to carry on dealing with the "real world."

The U.N. effort to construct global strategies concerning the great issues of our time attempts to convince the political order that a common security agenda is the only way the world will survive and become a safe place for all its differences. The old idealism is, in fact, the new realism. What morality as expressed in the past by religions told us we should do for one another, the pragmatics of survival in the modern age tell us we must do.

Remembering that the U.N. is an association of governments (and not an entity of its own), the fact that governments have recognized the need of an agenda for human security is a hopeful sign for the future. That this agenda has even been constructed without public demand stirred up by the powerful instruments of business and the media is perhaps a small miracle. The trend line of history, in which the advanced sections of civil society are prodding governments to take steps for the common good, is revealed.

The long history of the world, characterized by the quest for domination, has reached a higher plateau where, for the first time, the mingling of intellectualism, technology, and danger provide both motivation and means for common survival. It is this very ability to assess the human condition that provides civil society with its new power.

The birth of a global consciousness is occurring despite the obdurateness of upholders of the old disorder. Business should be a chief midwife, since commerce has benefited enormously from the speed of electronic transactions in the global marketplace. The media, ever searching for the fascinating, have a new world of dramatic information to impart.

Those who have been enriched by the past resent the intrusion of a problematic future on the comforts of the present. The present, however, is not sustainable. The political process, the way in which we measure progress, must be changed. Democracy and the common good must now be fitted together on global terms.

A national—and global—debate is necessary to put a spotlight on the survival issues. Academics, religious leaders, women's groups, and the other leading components of civil society all have a vital role to play in bringing forward information and opinions. We live at the most dynamic moment in world history. We are not prisoners of the past. We are creators of the future.

A New Medium, A New Message

10

Civil society activists today bypass the mainline media. That itself ought to be a big story!

The power derived from using the new communications technology—the Internet, e-mail—has had astounding results in mobilizing nongovernmental organizations. Huge amounts of information on social justice themes are now available at the click of a mouse. We are, in effect, our own editors.

The International Campaign to Ban Landmines, a world-wide coalition of NGOs that stimulated public support for the Landmines Treaty, traced its success to a constant electronic exchange of information—both internally among its own members as well as with governments, the media, and the general public. The Multilateral Agreement on Investment (MAI), which bureaucrats in the OECD countries were trying to slip through without much public attention, was defeated, for now, by public protests generated by an e-mail campaign. Computer networks supporting the indigenous Zapatista rebellion in the Mexican state of Chiapas evolved from providing information on human rights abuses by the police into an electronic fabric of opposition to much wider abusive economic policies. In Canada, networks of NGOs in the disarmament, development, environment, and human rights fields are all using e-mail list servers to provide real time information and documentation that would otherwise be missed.

Modern communications technology has become the driving force behind the "new diplomacy" that brings together the tiers of grassroots, national, and supranational organizations. It is perhaps the greatest facilitator in the establishment and strengthening of an effective civil society. The Internet nourishes the involvement of those who seek change and creates a momentum of interests and ideas. It enables citizens and groups to participate in the political affairs and policy-making processes of their country that never would have been possible with the corporate controlled exchange of information.

The egalitarian nature of the Internet—the initial costs of setting up a home computer and going on-line are admittedly high—has opened up a new era for grassroots organizations struggling to make themselves heard. Where low-budget organizations once took weeks to generate a few hundred letters or phone calls into a government department, they can now mobilize thousands of members almost instantly.

The potential of the Internet as an educational tool has barely been tapped. It is still uncertain just how powerful it can be in affecting government policies or effecting new legislation. The lobbying power of big business is an enormous force to be challenged.

Nor is the Internet a blessing without blemish. The information superhighway can transport the best, but it can also transport the worst. Hate speeches, child pornography, racist propaganda, and tips for would-be terrorists have moved onto the Internet. Dislodging the vilest material gets into the familiar arguments of civil libertarians for free speech and charges of censorship. Software programmers are finding ways to prevent certain websites from being accessed by children. But in the end, society will have to decide what it will tolerate and allow in the evil use of this great technology—just as it grapples with how much it will allow the same technology that can prolong lives to be used to create weapons of mass destruction. Global society is not yet morally mature enough to ban the worst of weaponry. It is not likely it will come to an agreed position, at least for some time to come, on precisely what will be disallowed on the Internet, access to which can be beamed up from any spot in the world.

The good that can be generated by the Internet is vastly greater than its dark side. And it is this good that has been seized on by NGO strategists to change the equations of power and challenge the conventional channels of communication by disseminating influence in the broadest possible fashion. The new information technology is particularly suited to the empowering of new groups and reshaping the constellation of international players.

The ease and speed of e-mail communication gives a feeling of "liveness" to communication around the country or the world in real time despite time zone changes. Its lower costs and increased reliability relative to telephone and fax facilitate communication with campaigners in widely separated geographic areas. It forms a community of concern that interacts with one another, generating ideas and plans. This changes the dynamics of citizen involvement in government and raises the level of sophistication in dealing with government departments and bureaucracies.

The International Campaign to Ban Landmines pointed out that electronic communication by itself did not "move the movement." Equally important was networking through travel and the development of personal relationships. The close working cooperation between NGOs and like-minded governments that developed into the Ottawa Process depended on regular face-to-face meetings. Personal contact can seal alliances. That is why the G8 meet every year at the Summit level; leaders get to know one another and build up their political capital through personal relationships. If the U.N. Security Council met at the Summit level once a year, it too would be much more effective. Teleconferencing is in vogue and it has undoubted benefits in conducting meetings when it is not convenient for participants to physically meet. But, government or nongovernment, the energy created when people gather and inter-act produces the will to act.

The Internet, however, ties individuals and groups together on a regular basis. It provides instant information and analyses. It was once arduous, if not impossible, to get United Nations documentation; now that material is readily available to substantiate positions. For example, the U.N. maintains on-line databases on human rights abuses. NGOs monitoring their government's compliance with human rights treaties can access information never before made universally available. The sheer speed and force of this communication makes the individual participant a stronger player. Shared values and partnerships develop.

Electronic Views on an Earth Charter

The enhanced electronic ability for civil society to participate in current events comes just at the moment when two other global trends have surfaced: increasing democratization and the growing importance of global governance. Information technology thus contributes to the reorganizing of international politics and makes possible a new concentration on developing social justice issues.

One of the most outstanding examples of this new fusion of the medium and the message is the development of an unprecedented document called the Earth Charter. Efforts to develop a set of principles for ecological security began in 1972 when the international community gathered in Stockholm for the first U.N. Conference on the Environment. Since then, many groups and coalitions developed principles and values for sustainable development. In 1987, the Brundtland Commission called for a new charter to guide States in the transition to sustainable development. It was intended that the Earth Summit, held in Rio in 1992, would adopt an Earth Charter. This would be a people's agreement on a statement of ethical principles to guide the conduct of people and nations towards each other and the Earth to ensure a sustainable future. But governments could not agree on the content of such an ambitious document, and settled for a safer Declaration on Environment and Development.

Following the Earth Summit, two international NGOs, the Earth Council and Green Cross International, with the support of the Dutch government, joined forces to develop an Earth Charter. They hope to have it adopted by governments and NGOs in 2002 at the Rio+10 Assembly at the U.N.

The gradual development of the Earth Charter allows time for a broad consultation process as a basis for a universally acceptable charter. Consultations and valuing processes are now going on in 25 countries, using e-mail and Internet resources to communicate reactions back and forth on drafts and involve more elements of civil society to support the endeavour. The Earth Council uses on-line conferences with NGOs in Africa, Asia, and Latin America on a regular basis.

The appeal of the Charter is broad because it addresses the crisis of growing poverty, destruction of environmental life support systems, violence, and personal alienation from nature and society. The 16 principles are drawn from international law, science, philosophy, religion, and U.N. global conferences. The Charter recognizes that humanity's environmental, economic, social, cultural, ethnic, and spiritual problems and aspirations are inter-connected. It affirms the need for holistic thinking and collaborative, integrated problem solving. The principles embody the constant theme of this book: enduring peace requires the political application of a social justice agenda, to include arms reductions, economic and social development, environmental protection, and the advancement of human rights. The Hague Appeal for Peace themes, outlined in Chapter 4, become more politically realizable when they are examined in the light of the Charter's principles.

The preamble notes that dominant patterns of production and consumption are altering climates, degrading the environment, depleting resources, and causing a massive extinction of species. A dramatic rise in population has increased the pressures on ecological systems and has overburdened social systems. Injustice, poverty, ignorance, corruption, crime and violence, and armed conflict deepen the world's suffering. Fundamental changes in our attitudes, values, and ways of living are necessary. "The choice is ours: to care for Earth and one another or to participate in the destruction of ourselves and the diversity of life."

The principles follow:

1. *Respect Earth and all life.* This affirms respect for the inherent dignity of every person and faith in the intellectual, ethical, and spiritual potential of humanity.

2. *Care for the community of life in all its diversity.* This states that common responsibility takes different forms for different individuals and nations.

3. *Strive to build free, just, participatory, sustainable, and peaceful societies.* This recognizes that a decent standard of living for all and protection of nature are the true measure of progress.

4. *Secure Earth's abundance and beauty for present and future generations.* This accepts the challenge before each generation to conserve and improve natural and cultural heritage and to transmit it safely to future generations.

5. *Protect and restore the integrity of Earth's ecological systems.* This would manage the extraction of renewable resources such as food, water, and wood in ways that do not harm the resilience and productivity of ecological systems.

6. *Prevent harm to the environment as the best method of ecological protection.* This would establish environmental protection standards and monitoring systems with the power to detect significant human environmental impacts; and make the polluter bear the full cost of pollution.

7. *Treat all living beings with compassion, and protect them from cruelty and wanton destruction.* This should be directed especially to governments as guarantors of human rights.

8. *Adopt patterns of consumption, production, and reproduction that respect and safeguard Earth's regenerative capacities, human rights, and community well-being.* This would include establishing economic indicators that reflect the full environmental and social costs of human activities; rely increasingly on renewable energy sources such as sun, wind, biomass, and hydrogen; provide universal access to health care that fosters reproductive health and responsible reproduction.

9. *Ensure that economic activities support and promote human development in an equitable and sustainable manner.* In promoting the equitable distribution of wealth, this would ensure that communities and nations are assisted in developing the intellectual, financial, and technical resources to meet their basic needs, protect the environment, and improve the quality of life.

10. *Eradicate poverty as an ethical, economic, and ecological imperative.* This would start by relieving developing nations of onerous international debts; make clean affordable energy available to all, promote meaningful employment, establish fair and just access to land, natural resources, training, knowledge and credit.

11. *Honour and defend the right of all persons, without discrimination, to an environment supportive of their dignity, bodily health, and spiritual well-being.* This would secure the human right to potable water, clean air, food, security, and safe sanitation in urban and rural areas; establish racial, religious, ethnic, and socio-economic equality; protect indigenous peoples.

12. *Advance worldwide the cooperative study of ecological systems.* This would regulate emerging technologies regarding their environmental, health and socio-economic impacts; and ensure that the exploration and use of orbital and outer space supports peace and sustainable development.

13. *Establish access to information, inclusive participation in decision-making, and transparency, truthfulness, and accountability in governance.* This would secure the right of all persons to be informed about ecological, economic, and social developments that affect the quality of their lives; protect the freedom of association; and create mechanisms to hold governments, international organizations, and business enterprises accountable to the public for the consequences of their activities.

14. *Affirm and promote gender equality as a prerequisite to sustainable development.* This would establish the full and equal participation of women in civil, cultural, economic, political, and social life.

15. *Make the knowledge, values, and skills needed to build just and sustainable communities an integral part of formal education and lifelong leaning for all.* This would engage the media in the challenge of fully educating the public on sustainable development; provide youth with training in civil affairs; encourage the contribution of artistic imagination for sustainable development.

16. *Create a culture of peace and cooperation.* This would eliminate weapons of mass destruction, promote disarmament, and convert military resources toward peaceful purposes; practice nonviolence and implement strategies to prevent violent conflict; promote cross cultural and interreliglious dialogue.

The ambitious agenda of the Earth Charter,* bringing together the diverse components of sustainable development, leads inevitably to a culture of peace. The agenda recognizes that peace is the wholeness created by balanced and harmonious relationships with oneself, other persons, other cultures, and Earth itself.

Obviously, a long worldwide dialogue in search of common ground and shared values is required to change today's disjuncted political maze into harmonious public policies. Huge constituencies of support need to be developed around the world; the instant transfer of information through electronic communication is a powerful new force in laying the groundwork for the new culture.

The first visible manifestation of this new power of civil society will be the Millennium People's Assembly to be held at the United Nations in 2000. Secretary-General Kofi Annan intends to add to a Special Assembly of Governments a companion people's forum. The People's Assembly will put forward plans of action on the global issues, and try to formalize people's participation in the U.N. system. The Secretary-General has signaled a growing readiness of the U.N. system to acknowledge the indispensable role that civil society must play in global governance. People around the world are preparing for this historic event by utilizing a wide range of communication technologies and a series of linked and simultaneous events to gather and synthesize views of people in all regions. New electronic communications links are forging a sense of global community.

* Since the Earth Charter is a "work in progress," readers of this book may want to give their own comments as development continues. You can e-mail your views to <echarter@terra.ecouncil.ac.cr>.

The Millennium People's Assembly Network, building on the work of more than 2,000 NGOs affiliated with the U.N., intends to bridge the gap that has existed for a long time between people, governments, and the United Nations. The global forums stimulated by the Millennium People's Assembly will increase the impact of civil society on public policy. This process will break down the barriers between NGOs and government by building in civil society active participation in the decision-making processes of the U.N.

Some proponents of this vision promote the idea of electing representatives of civil society to attend an annual People's Assembly at the U.N., thus increasing further the power of civil society to effect change. The idea may not be so far-fetched, considering that the present European Parliament, where members are directly elected by citizens in respective countries, started by the appointment of delegates to a body that had no direct powers. Like the idea of world government, which may or may not ever arrive, a regular People's Assembly with the power to send resolutions forward to both the General Assembly and the Security Council may be a long way off. But it is clear that the day of governments deciding global policies by themselves behind closed doors at the U.N. is over.

The involvement of great numbers of NGOs in the U.N. conferences of the 1990s set the stage for an emerging global civil society that is now bound to strongly influence development of the human security agenda as the basis for peace in the 21st century.

The Earth Charter and The Hague Appeal for Peace brilliantly show how a regular People's Assembly at the U.N. could significantly advance the agenda for human security. There is today an undeniable forward movement by civil society in substantively addressing world issues, effectively communicating concerns, and mobilizing strength. Governments are still roadblocks; they still possess enormous power. But an awakening of a humanity concerned for its own survival is taking place. When this force gathers strength, it will become unstoppable.

Epilogue

A Long and Arduous Task

It happened that the week I started writing this book, NATO began its long bombardment of Serbia and Kosovo. Day after day, as the destruction, cruelties, and human suffering mounted before our eyes, it became apparent to me that militarism had run amuck.

At the outset, I stood in the Senate and opposed the bombing. I spoke at meetings across Canada. Since the five political parties in the House of Commons initially approved of Canada's participation in the war, I was at first a lonely voice on Parliament Hill. Gradually, parliamentarians started having second thoughts as they began hearing from constituents who were appalled at the continuing carnage.

At the beginning, I came under attack by those who took the position that the bombing was necessary to end the horrible ethnic cleansing perpetrated by the Slobodan Milosevic regime in Serbia. But soon I was hearing from people who wanted a political, not military, solution to the Kosovo crisis. I received more than 300 e-mails, faxes, and letters, which ran 71 percent in support of my position and 29 percent opposed (i.e., supporting the war). It became clear to me that many people in Canada were not taken in by the spurious arguments daily advanced by NATO spokesmen and relayed through the Canadian government system that NATO was doing the right thing by keeping up the military pressure on Milosevic.

When former U.S. President Jimmy Carter expressed his criticism of the NATO campaign, joining his dissent to growing fissures within the Alliance, U.S. policy began to shift. Carter said: "The decision to attack the entire nation has been counterproductive, and our destruction of civilian life has now become senseless and excessively brutal."

It took a long time for the expressions of outrage to sink in to the NATO leadership. Under the cover of retaliation for Serbian barbarism against the Kosovars, NATO was able to obscure the real issue: the future of international law.

The slaughter of innocent people in Kosovo, like similar horrors in Rwanda, Somalia, and Cambodia must be stopped by military force, if necessary, but only exercised by the U.N. Security Council. The Serbian parliament—before the bombing began—accepted a proposal to station U.N. forces in Kosovo to monitor a political settlement to the crisis. But it rejected the West's imposition of NATO troops alone in Kosovo. Negotiations broke down when they should not have. Human tragedies caused by the bombing multiplied. The situation for the Kosovars worsened many times over.

When U.N. Security Council Resolution 1244 was adopted on June 10, 1999, ending the Kosovo war, it provided for an international military and civilian presence "under United Nations auspices" to keep the peace. Moreover, the interim administration for Kosovo is "to be decided by the Security Council." NATO troops are a leading element of the international force, to be sure. But so are the Russians, a point the Russian government underlined through its quick deployment of troops into the area. It is a tragic irony that, after all the NATO blundering, the Kosovo war ended with an agreement that could have been reached before the bombing.

There are times when the use of force may be legitimate in the pursuit of peace, but unless the Security Council is restored to its pre-eminent position as the sole source of legitimacy on the use of force, the world is on a dangerous path to anarchy. NATO cannot be permitted to determine by itself when force will be used. Yet the NATO 50th Anniversary Summit, occurring shortly after the bombing began, took a deliberate decision to set itself up as the arbiter on when it would use force. The Russians and the Chinese will never accept a NATO-dominated world.

Already, the consequences of the Kosovo war have spread far beyond the human toll. The hopes for a cooperative global security system have been dashed on the rocks of power. The trust engendered during the supposed end of the Cold War is now shattered. New arms races are underway.

During the writing of the book, I went to the final preparatory meeting at the U.N. for the 2000 Review of the Non-Proliferation Treaty and observed, once again, the stalemate in nuclear disarmament. This time, the talk was of Russia and China reasserting nuclear weapons strength as a result of the Kosovo crisis. In fact, the whole non-proliferation regime is under siege today.

Nothing has more clearly demonstrated the non-proliferation crisis than the rejection of the Comprehensive Test Ban Treaty (CTBT) by the United States Senate. While domestic politics was cited as a chief reason for the failure of the CTBT ratification process in the Senate, the debate underscored the unilateralism that drives the U.S. Congress. Powerful forces in the U.S. are demanding national military superiority at the expense of world treaties to effect an enduring peace. This superpower domination, met by Russian, Chinese and Indian resistance, will lead to new nuclear arms races in the 21st century. Moreover, U.S. insistence on developing a ballistic missile defence system is actually stimulating more development of new nuclear weapons by the opponents of the U.S.

The world is staring into an abyss of nuclear weapons proliferation. The danger of the use of nuclear weapons is growing, as India and Pakistan have demonstrated. The recognition of this should galvanize intelligent and committed people—in both governments and civil society—to action.

Nuclear weapons, like the Kosovo war, are about the rule of law. How will international law be imposed in the years ahead: by the militarily powerful determining what the law will be, or by a collective world effort reposing the seat of law in the United Nations system?

The Kosovo war and the CTBT ratification breakdown have made even more urgent the themes of this book. A world of "bread not bombs" is certainly possible, but only if the international community is determined to build the conditions for peace. This is a long and arduous task. For my part, it is a task that will occupy the rest of my political life.

Notes

1. **The Poor Get Poorer**
   The Quality of Life Commission report "Listen to Me" (March 1996) is available through the Edmonton Social Planning Council, Suite #41, 9912–106 Street, Edmonton, Alberta, T5K 1C5. I have also drawn material from *The Growing Gap*, published by the Centre for Social Justice, 836 Bloor Street West, Toronto, Ontario, M6G 1M2, and *Our Neighbours' Voices: Will We Listen?* published by the Interfaith Social Assistance Reform Coalition (Toronto: Lorimer, 1998). The *Human Development Report,* published annually by the U.N. Development Programme, contains excellent analyses of world poverty conditions.

2. **The Cold War Is Not Over**
   Statistics on war deaths in this century are contained in the *SIPRI Yearbook: Armaments, Disarmament, and International Security* (Oxford: Oxford University Press [published annually]) from the Stockholm International Peace Research Institute, Stockholm, Sweden. There is a great amount of detailed information concerning the effects of war on children contained in the U.N. study, "Impact of Armed Conflict on Children," conducted by Graça Machel, U.N. Document A/51/306, August 26, 1986. Information on the impact of modern agricultural crises on warfare is found in the study, "To Cultivate Peace: Agriculture in a World of Conflict," published in 1998 by the International Peace Research Institute, Oslo. The article by Michael Renner, "Ending Violent Conflict," in *State of the World 1999* (New York: W.W. Norton & Co., 1999 [published annually]) presents the effects of the global arms trade. Figures on U.S. arms spending are collated by the Center for Defense Information, Washington, D.C. The Advisory Opinion of the International Court of Justice, on the legality of nuclear weapons, is found at **www.icj-cij.org/icjwww/idecisions/isummaries/iunanaummary960708.htm** The New Agenda Coalition's 1998 resolution calling for nuclear weapons negotiations is found at **www.middlepowers.org/documents/nac.html**.

3. **Where Bread and Bombs Intersect**
   Facts about military spending in India and Pakistan are contained in *Human Development in South Asia* 1997 (New York: Oxford University Press, 1998 [published annually]). Contrasting figures about what the world spends on defence and economic and social needs are contained in *GAIA: An Atlas of Planet Management,* Norman Myers, ed. (New York: Anchor Books, Doubleday,

1993). The Inga Thorsson study is found in *Disarmament and Development: Declaration by the Panel of Eminent Personalities*, U.N. Publications, 1986. See also *Final Document: International Conference on the Relationship Between Disarmament and Development*, U.N. Publications, 1987. "The Brussels Call for Action," containing the findings of the 1998 International Conference on Sustainable Disarmament for Sustainable Development, can be obtained from Project Ploughshares, Conrad Grebel College, Waterloo, Ontario, N2L 3G6. U.N. Under-Secretary-General Jayantha Dhanapala's comments are contained in his address to the Brussels conference.

4   **Towards a Culture of Peace**
The Global Action to Prevent War program is directed by Ambassador Jonathan Dean, Dr. Randall Forsburg, and Professor Saul Mendlovitz, c/o Institute for Defense and Disarmament Studies, 675 Massachusetts Avenue, Cambridge, Massachusetts, 02139. I have also drawn from "Preventing Deadly Conflict," the report of the Carnegie Commission on Preventing Deadly Conflict, Carnegie Corporation of New York, 1979 Massachusetts Avenue, N.W., Suite 715, Washington, D.C., 20036–2103. Helpful material on the development of a culture of peace is contained in "Preliminary Consolidated Report to the United Nations on a Culture of Peace," UNESCO, Document 155ex/49, Paris, August 11, 1998. The Hague Appeal for Peace has a website at www.haguepeace.org or can be reached c/o IALANA, Anna Paulownastraat 103, 2518 BC The Hague, The Netherlands, tel. 31.70.363.4484. Material on the Middle Powers Initiative can be obtained from MPI, 727 Massachusetts Avenue, Cambridge, Massachusetts, 02139.

5   **The Right to Human Development**
An Agenda for Development, submitted to the United Nations by former Secretary-General Boutros Boutros-Ghali in 1994, U.N. Document A/48/935, addresses economic growth, trade, finance, science and technology, poverty eradication, employment, and human resources development. It also deals with the role of democracy, human rights, the role of civil society, the empowerment of women, and good governance. Material on the Social Summit in Copenhagen is found in "The World Conferences: Developing Priorities for the 21st Century," U.N. Publication E.97.I.5. The Development Assistance Committee's report, "Shaping the 21st Century: The Contribution of Development Cooperation" is published by the OECD, Paris. The United Nations Development Programme's study, "Integrating Human Rights with Sustainable Human Development," is a helpful resource. Material on the Tobin tax is available from The Halifax Initiative website www.sierraclub.ca/national/halifax/, a coalition of environment, development, social justice, and faith groups.

6   Pushing Equitable Global Standards
A study of all the factors involved in U.N. reform is contained in Richard A. Falk, Samuel S. Kim, and Saul H. Mendlovitz, eds., *The United Nations and A Just World Order* (Boulder: Westview Press, 1991). The Beijing Declaration and Platform for Action, U.N. Document A/CONF.177/20, adopted by the Fourth World Conference on Women, 1995, can be found at www.igc.org/beijing/un/.

7   Justice Both Legal and Social
The Canadian Ecumenical Jubilee Initiative's website at: www.web.net/~jubilee/ is a good source for the expression of social justice themes in practical terms. The Other Economic Summit's website (known as the People's Summit), pender.ee.upenn.edu/~rabii/toes/, monitors the performance of the G8 and issues alternative economic agendas.

8   Canada: The U.N. and/or NATO?
Canada's nuclear weapons policies are contained in documentation released by the Government on April 19, 1999 and found on the Internet at dfait-maeci.gc.ca/nucchallenge/menu-e.htm. The Project Ploughshares 1998 report, "Nuclear Weapons, The Problem, The Solution, Canada's Role," examines the state of Canadian public opinion on nuclear weapons. An assessment of Canada's performance in implementing environment policies is found in the House of Commons Environment and Sustainable Development Committee Report, *Enforcing Canada's Pollution Laws: The Public Interest Must Come First! Canadian Environmental Protection Act enforcement study* (tabled in the House of Commons, May 25, 1998).

9   Media, Politics and the Corruption of Values
Information on the attempt to devise a "new world information order" is found in a Briefing Paper, 1983, published by the United Nations Association in Canada. The publications of Fairness and Accuracy in Reporting, 130 W. 25th Street, New York, N.Y. 10001, are useful in assessing the media's performance. "How Mass Media Destroy Activism—and Five Ways to Turn It Around," by Peter Mann in *WHY* (World Hunger Year, 505 Eighth Avenue, 21st Floor, New York, N.Y. 10018–6582, Winter 1998, no. 30) deals with ways civil society can use the media.

10 A New Medium, A New Message
The Earth Charter and related material can be found at: www.earthcharter.org. The Millennium People's Assembly has a website: www.worldgov.org/MPAN/.

Appendix

Informative Websites

A great deal of the information in these pages was obtained through instantaneous access to documents, initiatives, and activities of organizations and groups whose efforts seek to change the priorities of public policy.

The dissemination of information furnished by the Internet is a powerful mechanism for social change. The Internet is a tool to increase the scope of knowledge, to extend the reach of information sharing, and to provide more individuals access to vast storehouses of analyses, data, and resources. It promotes increased communication and interaction among specialists with a variety of interests in an array of fields.

The following, in alphabetical order, are websites that proved valuable in writing this book.

Canadian Ecumenical Jubilee Initiative
L'Initiative oecuménique canadienne pour le Jubilé
www.web.net/~jubilee

The Canadian Ecumenical Jubilee Initiative is a project of 30 churches and ecumenical organizations seeking renewal for the world through the release from debt bondage (including the Jubilee 2000 debt campaign), the redistribution of wealth, and the renewal of the Earth. The Initiative integrates concerns for social justice, peace, and ecological integrity.

Canadian International Development Agency
Agence canadienne de developpement international
www.acdi-cida.gc.ca/index.htm

Canadian International Development Agency (CIDA) delivers Canada's official development assistance programs, supporting sustainable development, fighting poverty and disease, as well as confronting other threats to human security in order to contribute to a more secure, equitable, and prosperous world. CIDA seeks to contribute to Canada's political and economic interests abroad by promoting social justice, international stability, and long-term relationships for the benefit of the global community.

Canadian Mission to the United Nations
www.un.int/canada/

This is a valuable asset for information concerning the policy issues both confronted and espoused by Canada in its seat on the Security Council. There are detailed and informative discussions of Canadian initiatives that include the protection of civilians in armed conflict, anti-personnel landmines, peace–building, and sustainable development.

Carnegie Endowment for International Peace, Non-Proliferation Project
www.ceip.org/programs/npp/

The Non-Proliferation Project is one of the pre-eminent sources of analysis, commentary, and surveillance of non-proliferation issues. An independent source of information, the Project conducts a wide array of professional and public-education activities promoting international efforts to curb the spread of weapons of mass destruction. The site includes press briefings, seminars, and proliferation policy briefs.

Centre for Defense Information
www.cdi.org/

Centre for Defense Information (CDI) is a private, nongovernmental, research organization in Washington, D.C., believing that strong social, economic, political and military components, along with a healthy environment contribute equally to a nation's security. The site includes valuable links that includes its publication, *The Defense Monitor*.

Earth Charter
www.earthcharter.org/

The Earth Charter gives expression to the principles of an integrated ethical vision for our common future. The site includes a background of the Charter, questions and answers, as well as Global Ethics, Sustainable Development and the Earth Charter, and an on-line academic conference held April 6–9, 1999 at www.earthforum.org. The principles espoused by the Charter clarify humanity's shared values in developing a new global ethic for a sustainable way of life.

Faith and the Economy
www.faith-and-the-economy.org/

Through this website, you may access a wide variety of resources, consultation papers, related links, and participate in discussions on issues related to social justice and the common good. Themes include poverty, homelessness, health, and education within both a Canadian and a global context.

The Hague Appeal for Peace
www.haguepeace.org/

The Hague Appeal for Peace is one of the best examples of the partnerships that are possible between citizens, governments, and international organizations. This "new diplomacy" will foster new approaches toward peace by concentrating on: international humanitarian and human rights law and institutions; conflict prevention and regulation; disarmament and human security; defining the root causes of war; and fostering a culture of peace for the 21st century.

Halifax Initiative
www.sierraclub.ca/national/halifax/

The Halifax Initiative is a coalition of nongovernmental organizations committed to the environment, development, and social justice. The network is concerned with the policies and practices of the international financial institutions and committed to their fundamental reform. The site offers links to members and associate members of the Coalition, including: Canadian Council for International Cooperation, North-South Institute, Oxfam-Canada, and the Sierra Club of Canada to name only a few.

Human Rights Internet
www.hri.ca/

Human Rights Internet (HRI) is dedicated to using its Internet presence to spread information and documents of the international human rights community. As a research tool, HRI allows you to search for new documents and publications in your area of interest, and learn about important and upcoming international human rights events and issues. HRI is a valuable launchpad into the widespread human rights community that exists on the Internet.

Middle Powers Initiative
www.middlepowers.org/

Middle Powers Initiative (MPI) is a network of international citizens' organizations encouraging the leaders of the Nuclear Weapon States to move rapidly to a nuclear weapon free world. The MPI seeks to press the NWS to start immediate multilateral negotiations leading to a Nuclear Weapons Convention, similar to the enforceable global treaty prohibiting and eliminating chemical weapons. The site contains important documents, such as *Towards a Nuclear Weapon Free World: The Need for a New Agenda*, the New Agenda Coalition Resolution at the United Nations, and the MPI Briefing Book.

NGO Committee on Disarmament
www.igc.apc.org/disarm/

The NGO Committee, operating at the United Nations, New York, is an independent service organization for disarmament issues. It provides updates from the newspaper *Disarmament Times*, the ABCs of Disarmament, and events and calendar information. It offers open channels for communication between citizens' groups, government and U.N. bodies.

Nuclear Age Peace Foundation
www.wagingpeace.org
www.napf.org/abolition2000/

The Nuclear Age Peace Foundation is an international education and advocacy group dedicated to issues of international peace and security. The Foundation performs research and analysis on critical issues of peace and global survival, and prepares and distributes educational materials by leading thinkers on these issues. It is recognized by the United Nations as a Peace Messenger Organization.

Parkland Institute
www.ualberta.ca/~parkland/

Based at the University of Alberta, the Institute brings together the academic and nonacademic communities to study public policy issues from a political economy perspective. The Institute involves those who are engaged in interdisciplinary and socially-engaged thinking, publishes research and provides informed commentary on economic, social, cultural, and political issues facing Albertans and Canadians.

Physicians for Global Survival
www.pgs.ca

An outstanding and comprehensive site with many categories: arms, war, peace, health, human dignity, landmines. Its section on the World Court Project and Abolition 2000 open into a wide range of information on the ramifications of the World Court's Advisory Opinion and the documents and activities of the citizens' movement to get negotiations for a Nuclear Weapons Convention completed by 2000.

Project Ploughshares
www.ploughshares.ca/

Canada's ecumenical peace research organization specializes in Canadian themes and provides back issues of the quarterly publication, *The Monitor*. The site provides text of submissions to the Parliamentary Committee reviewing Canada's nuclear weapons policies, the annual *Armed Conflicts Report*, working papers and briefings promoting disarmament and demilitarization, the peaceful resolution of political conflict, and the pursuit of security based on equity, justice, and a sustainable environment.

Stockholm International Peace Research Institute
www.sipri.se/index.html

Stockholm International Peace Research Institute (SIPRI) is one of the most important resources for research in the field of military spending, disarmament and international security. The aim of the Institute is to foster an understanding of the conditions for peaceful solutions to international conflicts and for a stable peace. The website includes highlights from all its past yearbooks, information on past conferences and lectures, and a great deal of other related links to numerous sites concerning peace and disarmament research.

The Other Economic Summit
pender.ee.upenn.edu/~rabii/toes/

The Other Economic Summit (TOES) is part of an international nongovernmental forum for the presentation, discussion, and advocacy of economic ideas and practices upon which a more just and sustainable society can be built—"an economics as if people mattered." TOES holds its own summits bringing together a broad alliance of NGOs that meets parallel to the annual G8 summits.

United Nations
www.un.org

The U.N. website renders an invaluable, wide-ranging view of the challenges facing the international community. Its search engine provides essential material concerning peace and security, economic and social development, international law, human rights and humanitarian affairs. Many documents and current news releases are available, as are links to the International Criminal Court and the International Court of Justice.

Worldwatch Institute
www.worldwatch.org/

The Worldwatch Institute's goal, through the conduct of inter-disciplinary nonpartisan research, is to foster the evolution of an environmentally sustainable society—one in which human needs are met in ways that do not threaten the health of the natural environment or the prospects of future generations. It is a tool for policymakers and the public for understanding global problems and trends.

Acknowledgments

The political stands expressed in this book are what I brought to the Senate. They were developed over a lifetime in journalism, politics, diplomacy, and education. Therefore the sources of my inspiration and help embody far more individuals than those who helped me with this project. The philosopher Jacques Maritain, the theologian Dietrich Bonhoeffer, and Mahatma Gandhi, in my view the greatest figure of the 20th century, head a long list of those who formed my thinking. Three men, the Nobel laureate Joseph Rotblat, the nuclear disarmament expert Bill Epstein, and the social activist-journalist Gary MacEoin continue to influence me.

I was helped in the preparation of this book by the Library of Parliament and its Research Branch, directed by Hugh Finsten.

My own research assistant Christopher Hynes found important statistics, organized my material, and researched the list of informative websites for the Appendix. His feedback was indispensable in the preparation process.

Pam Miles-Séguin, my secretary for many years when I was a Member of Parliament, rejoined my professional life when I was named a Senator, and, as Administrative Assistant, continually clears the path for me to work in two cities, Edmonton and Ottawa, at the same time. She diligently prepared the manuscript.

I have also received ongoing assistance from Bonnie Payne, my assistant in Edmonton, and Jennifer Radford, my former student and intern in my Ottawa office.

Khalid Yaqub, also a former student and an expert in computer sciences, prepared the graphs used in the book, as he did my Senate website.

The manuscript was improved by the comments offered by Ernie Regehr and Bill Robinson of Project Ploughshares and

Jim Wurst, former editor of *Disarmament Times* at the United Nations. Staff at Project Ploughshares also provided important information as did staff of the Parkland Institutue. Any remaining errors in the book are my responsibility.

Ruth Bertelsen, as she has with my previous books, gave me the confidence to proceed with this one. I am grateful to Glenn Rollans and the University of Alberta Press for, once again, publishing one of my works, and to Mary Mahoney-Robson for her editing and caring approach to my work. Carol Berger prepared the final index and Ana Herrera designed the book.

I thank Dr. Janine Brodie, Chair of the Political Science Department, University of Alberta, for her support of my teaching, now in the eleventh year at the university.

Finally, there is a group of people, members of the International Steering Committee of the Middle Powers Initiative, who have a profound influence on my work, and whom I wish to thank: Michael Christ, Senator Alan Cranston, Kate Dewes, Jonathan Granoff, Rob Green, David Krieger, Ron McCoy, Bruna Nota, Suzy Pearce, Jennifer Simons, Alice Slater, Fernando de Souza Barros, Maj-Britt Theorin, Alyn Ware, and Peter Weiss.

Edmonton
Fall 1999

Index

media, xii, 117–26
 new media, 127–36
Mexico
 Chiapas rebellion, 22, 127
 New Agenda Coalition, 30
 Non-Proliferation Treaty, 29
Middle Powers Initiative (MPI), x,
 142, 149
military conflict, 19–46, 101–15
military expenditures, world, 37, 40,
 44
Milosevic, Slobodan, 91
Mozambique
 child soldiers, 20
 war, xi, 56
Multilateral Agreement on
 Investment (MAI), 127

Nagasaki, 27, 30
Namibia, 56
National Anti-Poverty Organization
 (NAPO), 10
NATO, 27, 104, 111, 122
 arms expenditure, 24–25
 Iraq, 88
 Kosovo and Serbia, 46, 49, 88,
 101–3, 114, 137–39
 nuclear weapons, 28, 30–31,
 106–15
Netherlands
 aid to developing world, 16
 Earth Charter, 131
New Agenda Coalition (NAC), 30,
 51, 107
New International Economic Order
 (NIEO), 68
New Zealand and New Agenda
 Coalition, 30

NGO Committee on Disarmament,
 149
Nicaragua and World Court, 89
Nicholas II, Czar of Russia, 58
Niger, 22
Nobel Peace Prize, 104
"Non-Nuclear Weapons States"
 (NNWS), 26–31
Non-Proliferation Treaty (NPT),
 27–29, 51, 87–88, 104, 107,
 111, 139
North Korea
 arms expenditures, 25
 nuclear weapons development, 29
Northern Ireland, xi, 56
Norway, aid to developing world, 16
Nuclear Age Peace Foundation, 149
nuclear weapons, x–xi, 26–31, 41,
 43, 50–54, 106–15, 139. See
 Non-Proliferation Treaty
"Nuclear Weapons States" (NWS),
 26–31, 51, 93, 107–9
 World Court, 89

Oberg, Lyle, reaction to Roche
 Senate speech, 7
Official Development Assistance
 (ODA), 16, 25, 36–37, 43, 68–69
 as percentage of GNP, 15
 vs. world military expenditures,
 36
Oppenheimer, Tamar, 104
Organization for Economic
 Cooperation and Development
 (OECD), 15–16, 25, 127, 142
 Development Assistance
 Committee, 43

Organization for Security and
Cooperation in Europe, 52, 101
Ottawa Process to Ban Landmines,
61

Pakistan
military spending, 141
nuclear weapons, 26, 28, 35, 79,
107
Palme, Olof, 39
Parkland Institute, 7–8, 150
Partial Test Ban Treaty, 85
Pearson, Geoffrey, 104
Pearson, Lester B., 104
Perez de Cuellar, Javier, 70
Peru, income distribution, 14
Philippines, 56
Physicians for Global Survival, 150
Poland and NATO, 27
poverty. *See* development
Alberta, 3–9
Canada, xi, 9–14
developing world, 14–17, 33–35,
63–64
cuts in aid to, 16
debt, 16–17, 66–68, 81, 96–97
Presidential Directive 60, 29
Project Ploughshares, 111–12,
142–43, 150

Qatar, opposition to the
International Criminal Court, 92
Quality of Life Commission, 3–6,
141

Rae, Saul, 104
Red Cross, 16
Reform Party and the Senate, xiii,
6–7
Rio Summit, 106
Russia, 79, 102–3, 138
arms expenditure, 24–25
arms trade, 23
income distribution, 14
nuclear weapons, 27, 29, 53, 107,
139
poverty, xi
U.N. Security Council, 78
Rwanda
crimes against humanity, 90
Tribunal, 91–92
war, xi, 19, 55, 102, 138

Security Council. *See* United
Nations, Security Council
Senegal, 22
Serbia, xi, 46, 49, 88, 101–3, 114,
137–39
Sierre Leone, 19
Sinclair, Adelaide, 104
Slovenia and New Agenda Coalition,
30
Social Development Summit, 61,
142
Somalia, xi, 19, 49, 55, 102, 138
South Africa, 56
income distribution, 14
New Agenda Coalition, 30
South Korea
arms expenditure, 24, 103
IMF, 96

About the Author

SENATOR DOUGLAS ROCHE, O.C.

Author, parliamentarian and diplomat, Douglas Roche was appointed to the Senate of Canada September 17, 1998. Senator Roche was Canada's Ambassador for Disarmament from 1984 to 1989. He was elected Chairman of the United Nations Disarmament Committee, the main U.N. body dealing with political and security issues, at the 43rd General Assembly in 1988. Senator Roche was elected to the Canadian Parliament four times, serving from 1972 to 1984 and specializing in the subjects of development and disarmament. In 1989, he was appointed Visiting Professor at the University of Alberta, where he teaches "War or Peace in the 21st Century?" He is an Officer of the Order of Canada, Chairman of Canadian Pugwash, and Chairman, Middle Powers Initiative, a network of eight international nongovernmental organizations specializing in nuclear disarmament. He is the author of fifteen previous books, and has contributed chapters to eight more. His most recent publications include *The Ultimate Evil: The Fight to Ban Nuclear Weapons* (1997) and *A Bargain for Humanity* (1993). In 1998, the Holy See named him a Knight Commander of the Order of St. Gregory the Great for his service as special adviser on disarmament and security matters.

Douglas Roche's Home Page on the Internet can be found at **www.sen.parl.gc.ca/droche.** He can also be reached by e-mail at: roched@sen.parl.gc.ca